Symbols

FOR OUR STUDENTS

at California College of the Arts

THE MONACELLI PRESS

Symbols: A Handbook for Seeing

MARK FOX *and* ANGIE WANG

foreword STEVEN HELLER

principal photography MARK SERR

CONTENTS

nature

animate

human

man-made

abstract

COSMOS OF SIGNS

When exploring the expanse of signs and symbols, it becomes perfectly clear that each one has multiple interpretations. Each sign is a reflection or variant of another, and meanings multiply. From a very few erupts a whole cosmos. The universe of signs and symbols devised throughout the ages of human history is head-spinningly immense and forever expanding. It may be finite, but we still can't see its limit. Like the stars, some of these signs and symbols are likely to burn bright, fade, and die, destined to be adapted or replaced by new ones.

Every society, culture, and tribe has contributed some transformative symbolic icon, developed over time, that embodies greater significance and existential power than the literal image or thing itself. Carl Jung called these life-defining symbols "archetypes"—subconscious yet universal "primordial images" with collective resonance and deep psychic ramifications. In other words, human existence depends to a large extent on navigating and learning from signs and symbols. Our survival has depended on the instinctual and intellectual deciphering of visual cues, because they are the markers of caution and proscription, as well as of edification. Not surprisingly, many of these archetypes are the basis for and components of how corporations, institutions, political parties, social movements, and religions pictorially and wordlessly communicate or brand themselves to the world.

As designers who specialize in trademarks, Mark Fox and Angie Wang work intensely in the realm of symbolism, and their years of experience and research have driven them to the task of identifying, categorizing,

OPPOSITE
The mapping of a metaphoric terrain is no less valuable than the mapping of a physical one. Both seek to orient, to locate the reader in a relational context. A relief map of the Crown Prince Islands, Disko Bay, Greenland. Created by Inuit fisherman Silas Sandgreen, painted driftwood on sealskin, 1925.

and explaining the multiple meanings of seminal archetypes. Some are so familiarly ingrained in our minds that we take them for granted; others contain so many alternative meanings that it can be difficult to fully comprehend their root symbolism. While neither a single book nor the entire interweb can contain every significant symbol, this book is a splendid and encompassing primer.

The daunting task of deciding which symbols to include, and what artifacts best represent them, might have given a case of vertigo to even the great interpreter of symbols, Joseph Campbell. This foundational and inspirational volume is all the more relevant in our digital age, when the references and meanings of common signs and the introduction of new icons and memes have fused into a fluid global language. Images in the collective unconscious have merged into a more popular cultural understanding. The classical and the commercial, the cultured and the crass, the high and the low, and every level in between—we have become symbol gluttons, and are engorged with marks that represent reality and fantasy. One sign invariably leads to another, forming a curiously woven web of symbols with alternative and sometimes contradictory meanings. Yet it is precisely how and why charged signs, like the swastika and serpent, at the same time signify such opposing realities—good and bad—that makes this study so compelling and important for the cause of visual literacy.

Signs and symbols are sometimes derived from an entity (or deity), or they are embraced by consensus of the mass. Or these processes become intertwined. My favorite example of this (although not addressed in this volume) is the crescent moon that was frequently cut into the doors of outdoor privies which, over time, became the universal symbol for an outhouse. As one of our most ancient and venerable cosmic symbols, its original range of meanings included the twenty-eight-day menstrual cycle, pregnancy, and fertility in general. Yet it was nineteenth-century cartoonists who transformed this into the comic symbol for the archetypal outhouse. In their entries for the *Moon* in this volume (page 29), Fox and Wang offer a range of yet more lunar associations, including fickleness, instability, and lunacy, based on the moon's mystical place in the heavens. My favorite reference is the phrase "pissing on the moon," a Dutch proverb warning against unattainable goals.

The meanings multiply. When contemporary designers, artists, or writers employ symbols to communicate messages, it is useful for them to know that some meanings can conflict with each other. That *Horns/ Antlers* (page 71), for example, can represent power and virility (the phallus), but also feminine generative powers—from whence comes the horn of plenty. Reading and comprehending signs and symbols can be as difficult as absorbing any new verbal and textual language. Interpreting—or projecting—a sign correctly, however, can mean the difference between praise and condemnation, success and failure, life and death. Very few signs and symbols are as crystal clear as the common roadway STOP sign, and the beauty of this book is showing that symbolic language is not concise and univocal, but fluid, contradictory, and richly endowed with narratives both past and present.

1 From a conversation between the authors and Aaron Betsky. Confirmed via email, June 29, 2015.

Around the time he organized the 1997 design exhibition "Icons: Magnets of Meaning" at the San Francisco Museum of Modern Art, curator Aaron Betsky observed, "An icon is a sign that has associational force to it. It's a spindle around which a lot of meanings and associations can turn."[1] We love this idea: the symbol as a focal point around which ideas are wound. It's a messy image, but then symbols are messy subjects; the meanings that cling to them can range from the perceptive to the preposterous—and can even be contradictory. The serpent, for example, is a symbol of evil, poison, and death, but it likewise represents medicine, healing, and life. Context determines a symbol's primary "read," of course, but it never fully subsumes the full array of its other meanings.

Our use of the word *symbol* is broad and inclusive. For our purposes, an image or artifact has symbolic value if it leads beyond itself; if it suggests an auxiliary narrative. Symbolic thought—the practice of using one thing to suggest another—is a fundamental human urge, and clearly an ancient one. Based on recent finds in South Africa's Blombos cave, it appears that humans have been generating symbols for at least 70,000 years, and possibly for millennia more. The invention of symbols—like the invention of tools—is one of the distinguishing features that separates humans from other animals.

In an article in the *New York Times,* science writer Ferris Jabr explores the relationship between symbols and tools, ultimately concluding that symbols *are* tools. Jabr describes the symbol as a kind of sensory enhancement: "Rather than directly changing the world around us,

OPPOSITE
A Hungarian flag stripped of the Soviet hammer-and-sickle during the 1956 Hungarian Revolution, documented by Austrian photographer Erich Lessing. Symbols can extend their meanings over time through a process of accretion. Even when erased or defaced, the symbol may simply fold the act of erasure into its layers of meaning.

2 Ferris Jabr, "Hunting for the Origins of Symbolic Thought," in *The New York Times Magazine,* December 5, 2014.

symbols change the way we perceive it. They extend not our bodies, but our minds."[2] If we apply Jabr's insight to the aphorism often attributed to Marshall McLuhan—"We shape our tools, and thereafter our tools shape us"—it yields a somewhat different truth. Namely, that it is our invention of symbols that makes us who we are.

And what forms do these symbols take? Our purpose in writing *Symbols: A Handbook for Seeing* is not simply to examine the competing narratives that envelop each symbol—there are many fine dictionaries of symbolism that already do this—but rather to document and celebrate the many ways in which designers and artists express symbolic ideas *visually*. One way we approach this task is via juxtaposition, through the shared space of the page on which images and artifacts from diverse times, places, and cultures can "converse." For instance, our *Hair* entry includes a 1967 poster of Bob Dylan, a seventeenth-century painting of the Gorgon Medusa, a photographic portrait of a young Tewa maiden, and a lock of hair preserved in a Victorian mourning brooch (pages 167–9). Hair is primarily a symbol of power, and these examples speak to different facets of that power: creative life force (Bob Dylan); brute power (Medusa); virginity and procreative potential (the Native American girl); or the immortality of the soul (hair as incorruptible matter).

This is our approach throughout. Works by well-known visual artists are intermixed with vernacular examples by unknown "makers"; media are varied and include architecture, painting, illustration, industrial design, graphic design, photography, sculpture, and indigenous arts.

Through purposeful recontextualization we seek to collapse some of the distinction between "high" and "low" visual culture, as well as to minimize the emotional distance between past and present. We believe that symbols are the embodiment of living ideas, even when the cultures that conceived them are no longer extant.

Finally, this is a visual guide to common symbols, not esoteric ones. We specifically chose to examine the narrative breadth and power of familiar signifiers *because* of their familiarity. How often do we think of doors in symbolic terms as we pass through them? Or consider the metaphoric capacities of the triangle or square? What we *think* we know we no longer truly see or fully appreciate—it appears that familiarity doesn't so much breed contempt as it does blindness.

Josef Albers distilled his approach to teaching with a fundmental desire: "I want the eyes to open."[3] Our hope is that, if we can succeed in defamiliarizing the familiar, we may nudge the curious to see anew.

Mark Fox & Angie Wang
San Francisco

3 From Nicholas Fox Weber, "'I Want the Eyes to Open': Josef Albers in the New World," in Achim Borchardt-Hume, ed., *Albers and Moholy-Nagy: From the Bauhaus to the New World* (London: Tate Publishing, 2006), p. 106.

SUN

MOON

STAR

LIGHTNING

FIRE

WATER

STONE

TREE

FLOWER

FRUIT

nature

SUN

As the "eye of the day" and of numerous sky gods, the sun is lidless, unblinking, all-seeing, and all-knowing. It is the eye of Zeus (Greek), of Ahura Mazda (Persian), of Varuna (Hindu), and of Odin (Scandinavian). The equivalence between sun, eye, and god is manifest in the glyph common to all three ideas: a central dot enclosed by a circle. The solar eye is so powerful, so piercing, that to fully meet its gaze would blind us. (See *Eye; Concentric Circles; Eagle*.)

The sun is central, the heart of the solar system. As the monarch is the heart of the empire, so the sun serves as an apt symbol of the monarch. The radiate crown—a circlet of gold from which points emanate—is a sun in miniature; to "wear" the sun is to confirm authority, if not divinity. The 17th-century reign of France's Louis XIV, the Sun King, exemplifies this symbolism. (See *Heart*.)

Since 671 CE the Japanese have referred to their archipelago as *Nihon,* "Origin of the sun." In Shinto, Japanese emperors were believed to be direct descendants of the sun goddess Amaterasu Omikami, and the current emperor still retains the vestigial title *Tenno,* or Celestial King. Japan's visual identity is largely solar: the national flag (the *Hinomaru*) is a red sun-disk; the naval ensign is a rising sun with sixteen rays; and the imperial standard features a sixteen-petaled golden chrysanthemum that represents the sun.

Sunlight illuminates and so denotes wisdom and truth. As the light of the sun falls equally on all, it is also a symbol of impartiality and justice.

1

2

1
Unlike the "fickle" moon, the sun's form is constant and unchanging. This fortune-telling card illustrated by Czech artist Vladimir Tesar in 1967 uses the steadfast sun to reinforce the theme of *Vernost* (Fidelity). Two lovers are joined by a safety pin, which may hint at a baby (and diapers) in their future. DETAIL

2
Circular forms featuring a central point with emanating lines can signify the sun and its radiance: the wheel; the sun wheel or sun cross; the swastika; the spider within its web; the flower. The rotational aspect of the swastika also emulates the diurnal path of the sun across the sky.

3

This Bwa dance mask was worn during agricultural ceremonies; the sun's life-giving rays are represented by a series of ser-rated, concentric rings. During Akhenaten's rule of Egypt, depic-tions of the sun-disk Aten show each ray terminating in a small cupped hand in offering. Burkina Faso, wood, 20th century.

4

Mao Tse-Tung, Chairman of the Communist Party of China, is envisioned as the radiant sun in this propaganda poster from the Cultural Revolution. The Chinese people were likened to sunflowers, obediently turn-ing their "faces" to follow the sun. *Resolutely Down With Liu Shaoqi!*, 1968. DETAIL

5

The Sundial Bridge in Redding, California, designed by Spanish architect Santiago Calatrava, 2004. The bridge's 217-foot pylon acts as a massive gnomon whose shadow indicates the hours of the day. Marked by the sundial, the sun's daily ascent and descent evokes a cycle of birth, death, and rebirth.

6

In the Occident the eye and sun are symbolic equivalents. German designer Willi Petzold uses a solar eye emanating golden rays to suggest the omniscience offered by medical advances in this 1930 poster stamp for the International Hygiene Exhibition in Dresden.

7

To the ancient Egyptians the obelisk formed a monumental ray of sunlight that symbolized the sun god Ra. The obelisk's apex is topped with a golden pyramid that is both solar and phallic. This particular obelisk was first erected c. 1200 BCE and is currently located in the Place de la Concorde in Paris, France.

8

The sun embodies clean energy in contrast to the radioactive toxicity of nuclear power. Danish activist Anne Lund's 1975 design "Nuclear Power? No Thanks" has become an international symbol of anti-nuclear protest. One of the sun's rays is subtly extended to suggest a solar speech bubble: the sun is the answer.

MOON

Our planet's only natural satellite waxes and wanes in its orbit, creating a cyclical rhythm that suggests birth (the emerging crescent); life (the full moon); death (the new moon); and rebirth (the return of the waxing crescent). The lunar cycle thus represents continuous regeneration and immortality.

As the moon doesn't generate its own light but merely reflects the glory of the sun, it is thought of as passive and, in patriarchal cultures, feminine. Its waxing or "growth" to fullness is linked to both agrarian fertility and impregnation, further extending the moon's *yin* associations. The female menstrual cycle corresponds so closely to the twenty-eight-day lunar cycle that it is called *menses,* Latin for "months."

The crescent moon with its two sharp points evokes cattle horns, a sign of power and male virility. (This masculine association only reinforces the moon's fertility symbolism.) Egyptian portrayals of Isis, for instance, feature the goddess wearing a headdress comprised of a sun nestled between crescent moon horns. In Christian iconography the Virgin Mary is often depicted standing on a supine crescent moon. (See *Bull; Horns/Antlers.*)

That the moon "appears" and "disappears" contributes to its association with fickleness and instability—in contrast to the steadfast sun. The inconstancy of the moon was believed to cause mental instability in humans, which is reflected in pejoratives such as *lunatic* and *moonstruck.*

OPPOSITE
This red bronze rabbit's "moon gazing" pose alludes to the Japanese folktale of a rabbit living on the moon, making rice-cake (*mochi*). In China, rabbit droppings are known euphemistically as "moon gaze." Japan, Meiji era.

2
A still from French filmmaker Georges Méliès' science-fiction fantasy *A Trip to the Moon* (1902). The moon is "the eye of the night"; landing a craft in its right eye leads to partial blindness and a diminution of its mythic (and romantic) identity.

3

"The Passing of the Eclipse," a satirical illustration by American caricaturist Udo Keppler for *Puck* magazine, 1904. In this context the moon (William Jennings Bryan) is a symbol of temporal ignorance, while the sun (Grover Cleveland) represents "Sane Democracy." DETAIL

4

A glyph of the waxing and waning moon by German artist and typographer Rudolf Koch, cut on wood by illustrator Fritz Kredel in 1923. This encapsulation of all the moon's phases "is symbolic of the vast and determinant influence of the Moon upon the life of man" [Koch].

5

The crescent moon enveloping a seven-pointed star, likely the planet Jupiter. Minted by Roman emperor Hadrian in 125–128 CE, its use would link the emperor with Juno (the Roman moon goddess) and Jupiter (the sky god), thus legitimizing his rule.

6

Until the latter half of the 20th century, the moon was seen as a quixotic, unattainable goal. Flemish painter Pieter Brueghel the Elder's 16th-century roundel of a man "Pissing on the Moon" illustrates a Dutch proverb that warns against futile endeavors. DETAIL

7
Ten years after the launch of
the USSR Luna 3 probe, the US
Apollo 11 successfully landed
on the surface of the moon. This
1969 photograph of an American
boot-print on lunar soil can be
seen as an imprimatur of ownership, rendering the moon a
"spoil" of the Cold War. DETAIL

8
A moon gate at the Summer
Palace in Beijing, China. A feature
of classical Chinese gardens,
the round portal is carefully
positioned to frame a view. This
is perhaps a playful reference
to moon-gazing, although this
"moon" might reveal a pond or
grove of trees.

9
The waxing phase of the moon
is associated with fertility and
growth, whether that growth
relates to crops or hair. (This
trademark from 1905 suggests,
"Trim the hair when the moon is
new.") Contemporary Farmers'
Almanacs still list the most
propitious days to plant crops
and cut hair.

STAR

Visible but unreachable, the star is a symbol of supremacy and celestial perfection. It represents an aspirational ideal.

The polestar—or North Star—is the pivot point around which the whole of the heavens appears to rotate. It was believed to be the center of the cosmos and the "door" to heaven; as a fixed point it symbolizes constancy and guidance. In China the polestar served as a metaphor for the emperor surrounded by his court; to the nomadic Buryats of Siberia, the stars encircling the polestar were seen as tethered horses.

The pentagram is a five-pointed star drawn in one continuous line; like the ouroboros, it suggests eternity. When plotted within a circle the star's five points occur every seventy-two degrees, effectively mapping the planet Venus' orbit over an eight-year period. To the Mesopotamians the circumscribed pentagram was identified with Venus as the morning and evening star—and symbolized the dual aspects of Ishtar as the goddess of both love and war.

The imposition of an equilateral triangle on its inverse creates the six-pointed star. Like *yin* and *yang,* this star is a union of opposites that embodies harmony and wholeness. To Hindus it is the coupling of the *lingam* and the *yoni;* in alchemy, it merges the male fire with the female water; as the Magen David, it represents Judaism. (See *Triangle.*)

An eight-pointed star symbolized Ishtar in her procreative role as the goddess of fertility and sex. The Moroccan Berber eight-pointed star represents female fecundity as well, and can be found on 20th-century knotted carpets.

1

1
This 14th-century *zillij* pattern incorporates the eight-pointed star known as *khatam* in Arabic. Translated as seal or last, in Islam *khatam* can refer to Muhammad, the "Last of the Prophets." On the tiled walls of the Alcázar of Seville, Spain, this stellar network may be understood as a proclamation of faith. DETAIL

2
When worn as a badge or used in a military context, the star signals supreme authority. The five-pointed star, in particular, is a favorite motif of the American, Chinese, and Russian militaries. This transnational adoption of the five-pointed star by competing militaries makes it a de facto "symbol of war" [Liungman]. A

Red Army stamp honoring "Red Officers' Day," issued by the Russian Socialist Federative Soviet Republic, c. 1918–22.

3
Paris' Place de l'Étoile (Place of the Star), redesigned by French civic planner Baron Haussmann in the 1860s. Twelve avenues radiate out from the Arc de Triomphe at the Étoile's center, creating a topographic "navel" for Paris that suggests the polestar.

4
The American state of Texas is known as the "Lone Star State" due to its history as a former independent republic. The motif of the single star is proudly embraced by Texans as a symbol of their state's exceptionalism. The trademark for Lone Star Donuts by American designer Rex Peteet, Sibley/Peteet Design , 1985.

5
The constellation Leo from Hyginus' *Poeticon Astronomicon,* a 1st-century star atlas published in Venice in 1482. Stars and planets were once believed to influence or even control human destiny, and so signified fate. Romeo and Juliet, Shakespeare's "star-crossed lovers," exemplify the reach of astral power. DETAIL

LIGHTNING

Lightning embodies multiple natural phenomena associated with notions of deity: light, heavenly fire, the thunderclap, and the explosive force of a bolt striking the earth. Its power is both procreative and lethal: inseparable from the vitalizing rain, but also from wanton destruction.

That it limns the sky so briefly—in the wink of the Thunderbird's eye, according to Native American legend—makes lightning a symbol of sudden insight and the revelation of truth. In Buddhism, the thunderbolt of the Buddha's teachings lays waste to ignorance, akin to the purifying properties of fire. (See *Fire.*)

The thunderbolt is an attribute of male storm and sky gods, among them Baal (Canaanite), Zeus (Greek), Jupiter (Roman), Thor (Norse), Indra (Indian), Shango (Yoruban), and Tlaloc (Aztec). These deities either personify lightning or wield it as a weapon—in which case it can take the form of a bolt, spear, arrow, hammer, *vajra,* or stone axe. As a vestige of its significance to speakers of Germanic languages, lightning is still honored on the fifth day of every week: Thursday, literally Thor's day, is Thunder's day. (See *Bow/Arrow; Hammer.*)

Some Native American and West African cultures made implicit comparisons between the undulations of serpents and the branching forms of lightning, as well as between their life-giving and life-taking symbolism. Prior to their destruction, "enormous brass pythons slithered head-first down the trapezoidal turrets" [Werness] of the royal palace of Benin, descending like metal thunderbolts. The python represented the *oba* (king), but it was also an emblem of the Benin god of death and lightning, Ogiwu. (See *Serpent.*)

1

1

Four pairs of lightning bolts flash from behind the name Telefunken in a trademark for the German pioneer of wireless telegraphy and radio. While the bolts are primarily visual cues for electricity—*funken* is German for "spark"—their arrangement is notable: the negative space formed by the convergence of each pair of bolts forms an arrow, one at each compass point. Like the fascist Arrow Cross, the overall effect is expansive, but in this context the arrows likely imply only the broad radio coverage achievable with Telefunken products. Vacuum tube packaging, West Germany, mid-20th century.

2

The Lightning Field is a work of land art by American sculptor Walter De Maria (1977). A grid of 400 stainless steel poles rise fifteen to twenty feet above the New Mexico desert, forming the tallest feature for miles. The result is an open invitation to lightning strikes. Photograph by John Cliett.

3

One of a system of wartime icons created for the US Citizens Defense Corps by American advertising designer Charles Coiner around 1942. When used on cloth armbands, this insignia identified civilian messengers. The bolt's two pointed ends suggest the speedy transmission—and reception—of messages.

4

Sanka hakuu, or *Rainstorm Beneath the Summit,* from the series Thirty-Six Views of Mount Fuji by Japanese artist Katsushika Hokusai. Flashes of red lightning signal that this sacred mountain is also an active volcano, with explosive power at its disposal. Woodblock print, c. 1826–33.

FIRE

Of the four classical elements—earth, air, fire, and water—fire is the only one that can be "made" by humans, thus conferring on mankind a power formerly reserved by gods. Fire is the terrestrial equivalent of the celestial sun, and it shares the sun's associations with illumination, wisdom, truth, and divine revelation. In Buddhist thought fire also symbolizes wisdom burning away ignorance. (See *Sun*.)

Fire breathes, moves, and consumes within a limited span of time. It lives and dies, and so represents life. Fire is also emblematic of the heart and its passions: love, lust, jealousy, hatred, wrath, and zeal. Its temperature reinforces these associations, and a flaming heart signals religious fervor in Catholic iconography. (See *Heart*.)

In ritual cremation as practiced in Hinduism, fire is an agent of purification and transmutation: it separates the material body from its immaterial (i.e. spiritual) essence. It is an act akin to burning a prayer written on paper, the words recast as smoke that then rises heavenward.

Like torrential rain or floodwaters, the destructive nature of uncontrolled fire is in contrast to its regenerative aspects—whether literal or symbolic. The infamous 1911 Triangle Shirtwaist Factory Fire of New York City, in which 146 garment workers died, ultimately served as a catalyst for the establishment of stronger worker protections and labor unions in America. (See *Water*.)

OPPOSITE
Tongues of fire—symbolizing the Holy Spirit—descend from heaven onto Christ's apostles at Pentecost. Solar fire is celestial and divine; by contrast, volcanic fire is subterranean and demonic, and fire generated by friction is considered carnal. Illuminated manuscript from Bavaria, Germany, c. 1030–40.

2
French anthropologist Claude Lévi-Strauss proposes in his book *The Raw and the Cooked* (1964) that cooking marks "the transition from nature to culture." Prometheus introduces the transformative gift of fire to mankind in this Paul Manship sculpture at Rockefeller Center, New York (1934).

3

A zinc "Fire Basket" designed by the Dutch studio Gebroeders Knip, 2001. The basket is comprised of "one-word poems" that encircle the fire and are in turn animated by it. The controlled fire is physically and symbolically central: a locus around which family and friends gather, and ideas are exchanged. This time-less relationship between fire and language is elegantly expressed by the Chinese word *tan,* meaning conversation, which is written by placing the character for "speech" alongside two stacked characters for "fire."

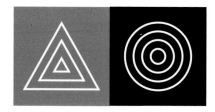

4
Fire has purifying properties, but the insatiable fire of Christian judgment signifies divine retribution. Hellfire (*infernus flamma*) issues from the maw of a great serpent in this panel from the Verdun Altar in Austria by French artist Nicholas of Verdun. Enamel with gilded copper, 12th century.

5
The belief that fire is the province of gods is persistent. Upon the detonation of the Trinity in 1945, American physicist J. Robert Oppenheimer recalled the words of the Hindu god Vishnu: "Now I am become Death, the Destroyer of Worlds." The atomic fireball from the later Castle Romeo weapons test, 1954.

6
The equilateral triangle, apex up, is a medieval sign for fire. (It is also associated with the sun, sun god, and erect phallus.) This trademark for the marketing firm Firewood pairs a triangle (for fire) with a stylized cross section of a log to denote wood. By American graphic designer Mark Fox, 2002.

7
The immortal phoenix rises from its pyre in this manuscript illumination from The Ashmole Bestiary. A universal symbol of cyclic resurrection, the phoenix's rebirth can only be catalyzed by the regenerative power of fire. England, parchment, 13th century.
DETAIL

WATER

Water is a universal symbol of life, especially so when it flows or "runs": springs, rivers, fountains, and seas. (American choreographer Twyla Tharp notes, "That is the definition of life: it moves.") Water that is frozen, stagnant, or brackish doesn't move and so suggests rigidity, disease, and lifelessness.

Rivers and large bodies of water create physical boundaries that set limits and define territory. The act of crossing a river or body of water, therefore, can serve as symbol of moving from one physical, mental, or metaphysical state to another. For the ancient Hebrews fleeing Egypt, crossing the Red Sea signaled a movement from slavery to freedom; for Julius Caesar and his army, crossing the Rubicon in 49 BCE marked a move from obedience and peace to insurrection and civil war. In Greco-Roman mythology, the dead cross the river Styx to reach the underworld, transitioning from life to afterlife. ("Many Rivers to Cross," the 1969 gospel-tinged hit from Jamaican reggae singer Jimmy Cliff, describes the stasis that results from an inability to "cross over.")

Water has metaphorical cleansing properties—"washing away" sins, for example—and this symbolism is at the heart of baptisms, ritual ablutions, and even floods. Because water was considered inherently "pure" in the Middle Ages, it was used in European witches' ordeals to determine guilt or innocence: if the accused floated, the woman was found guilty as her "impurity" had been rejected by the water. The recent revival of waterboarding (or "simulated drowning") by the CIA to torture detainees reinforces the symbolism of water as a morally purifying agent.

OPPOSITE
Open water suggests boundless potential. This sense of freedom even extends to small bodies of water when we swim in them: to swim is to defy gravity and, in some sense, to fly. *Sprung von 10m Turm*, from the 1936 Berlin Olympics recorded by German filmmaker Leni Riefenstahl.

2
The Japanese water sign known as *mitsudomoe* depicts a whirlpool or eddy. Typically featured on ceramic tiles positioned at the apex of roof eves, it functions as an apotropaic symbol to protect buildings from fire. Its form is reminiscent of the Aegean triskele.

3

While water is generally regarded as female, rain—the inseminating principle of the sky god—is one form of water that is specifically male. Three young Mexican boys dress as jaguars and a fox to petition the Jaguar god in a 1982 fertility and rainmaking festival with pre-Columbian origins.

4

Some waters are believed to possess spiritual or curative properties. Holy water—water that has been sanctified by a priest—has been used to expiate sins for centuries. The secular practice of medicinal bathing dates back even further, and early Roman sites include Bath, England, and Baden-Baden, Germany.

5

Deep water symbolizes the mysterious, the unknown, and the unconscious. What is concealed beneath the surface of water can easily trigger feelings of anxiety and dread. A torpedoed Japanese destroyer seen through the periscope of the USS Wahoo or USS Nautilus, 1942.

6

When in the form of a flood, water is a simultaneous destructive and regenerative force. In this 13th-century manuscript illumination depicting Noah and the Ark, the roiling floodwaters take the form of spirals, cyclical symbols of winding and unwinding, birth and death. DETAIL

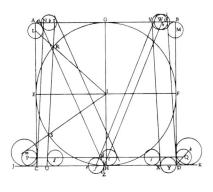

7
Illuminated lanterns float down a river in the *Toro nagashi* ceremony that marks the end of the Japanese *Obon* festival. Ancestral spirits, symbolized by lanterns, must return to their own world at the conclusion of the festival; the river serves as a metaphysical conduit to carry them back.

8
The form of the classical Roman letter *M* evolved from the Egyptian hieroglyph for water, and the zigzagging lines of moving water are still evident. American designer David Lance Goines' *A Constructed Roman Alphabet* (1982) examines the geometric basis of this serifed letter.

9
Much like the use of an "eternal flame" at the French Tomb of the Unknown Soldier (1920), American artist Maya Lin's Civil Rights Memorial (1998) uses water to further narratives of permanence and remembrance. The ceaseless flow of water over black granite is a reminder of the enduring ideals of racial equality.

STONE

Whether as one of the "bones" of Mother Earth or as a concentration of terrestrial energy, stone is an animist symbol of static life force. Stone preserves "heat, coldness, water and (as jewels) light" [Tresidder]. When carved, stone also preserves language and ideas; when inked—as in lithographic printing—stone not only preserves, it disseminates.

Its material permanence suggests incorruptibility, and in most ancient cultures stone was believed to possess apotropaic powers. Thus gravestones not only marked burial sites but protected the dead; in Germany the souls of the deceased were thought to indwell their gravestones.

Stones with a celestial provenance such as meteorites were—and continue to be—objects of especial veneration. Originating in the heavens, aeroliths were linked with both sky gods and with rain, and thus were emblems of great power and fertility. Accessing the stone's power was accomplished through ritual contact: touching, rubbing, or kissing. This practice survives in Islam where the faithful strive to touch or kiss the Black Stone embedded in the wall of the Ka'aba, no doubt because it is the metaphoric "right hand of Allah."

Lithophones are stones that resonate like bells when struck, and these musical rocks were presumably valued for their ability to transmit power through sound. (Some of the monoliths at Stonehenge in England have sonic properties.) The ancient Chinese believed that lithophones contained the life force *chi,* and they rang stone chimes as early as the Neolithic period. During the Qing dynasty, elaborately carved green jade chimes were prized as symbols of fertility and good fortune. (The Chinese word for "stone chime," *qing,* is a homophone of "celebrate.")

2

OPPOSITE
Rock is "living" when in its natural state. To carve a tomb out of living rock is, in some sense, to inter the dead in matter that contravenes death itself. The necropolis known as Al-Khazneh or The Treasury, Petra, Jordan, early 1st century CE. Autochrome, 1907 or later.

2
Its extreme hardness and brilliance make the diamond a symbol of material perfection, light, and life. By encrusting a platinum skull with diamonds, British artist Damien Hirst transforms our preeminent symbol of mortality into an imperishable object of desire. *For the Love of God,* 2007.

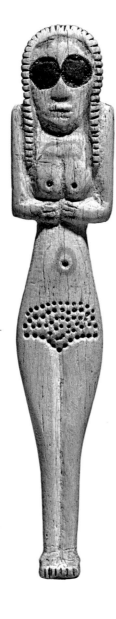

3
The blue gemstone lapis lazuli was highly prized in the ancient world as a symbol of the firmament and, by extension, sky gods. (The Latin *lapis* and Arabic *azul* translate to "stone sky.") Inlaying the eyes of this bone figurine with lapis lazuli implies otherworldy vision. Upper Egypt, Early Predynastic period, 4000–3600 BCE.

4
The Stone of Scone was the coronation seat for Scottish kings until it was stolen by the English—who subsequently built it into their own coronation chair in 1300–01. Crowning British monarchs on this stone symbolically justified the rule of England over Scotland for 700 years. Westminster Abbey, London, c. 1875.

5
This medieval alchemical sign for stone appears to depict an altar-like trapezoid of dressed stone. In a variation of this sign the bisecting, vertical stroke terminates in an arrowhead—perhaps suggesting that stone's power stems from the earth, below.

6
The Buddhist mantra *Om mani padme hum* blankets a rock formation above Namche Bazaar in Nepal. The stream of Tibetan script animates the landscape, as if the mountain itself were uttering the six-syllable prayer. The mantra's persistence as a devotional practice is perfectly suited to stone's material permanence.

TREE

The tree is animate but, being firmly rooted, is incapable of locomotion. This stability contributes to its role as an *axis mundi,* a world center whose roots link the underworld to the realm of men above, and whose branches link the heavens to the realms below. Pre-Columbian Mayans believed that the ceiba—a massive tree that lives hundreds of years and grows to over 200 feet— bridged these three realms of existence and served as a metaphysical "ladder" for the passage of gods from one world to the next. Chinese and Nordic myths record similar beliefs.

Like the serpent, which sheds its skin, or the moon, which wanes and waxes, the deciduous tree is a symbol of cyclical regeneration and renewal. The evergreen—always in leaf—symbolizes immortality and, in Asian cultures, longevity. (See *Moon; Horns/Antlers; Serpent.*)

In some religious traditions a Tree of Life grows in the center of Paradise, with four rivers issuing from its base. Its fruit (or sap) typically confers immortality or knowledge. The Bodhi Tree, the sacred fig integral to the Buddha's enlightenment, can be understood as a Tree of Life. Another expression of this motif is the inverted tree of Kabbala: with its roots outspread to the sky, the inverted tree signifies the nurturing and illuminating power of the sun descending from above. (See *Sun.*)

An exception to the tree as a symbol of life is the cross of crucifixion—known by Christians as "the tree"—and lynching trees, sites of extrajudicial mob killings. American jazz vocalist Billie Holiday sang of lynchings on "Southern trees" in the lament "Strange Fruit" in 1939.

2

OPPOSITE
The Pine of Success grew over the Sumida river in Edo and became a landmark for those traveling north by boat to the pleasure quarters of Yoshiwara. In Japan the pine tree symbolizes unrequited love; this particular pine represented carnal success. Woodblock print by an unknown Japanese artist, 1900–20.

2
Thought to derive from the Babylonian Tree of Light, the menorah's essential form is arborescent. This bronze coin displays a five-branched menorah, a variation of the more familiar seven-branched candelabra. Minted by the Umayyad Caliphate, possibly in Iliya (occupied Jerusalem), around 730–750 CE.

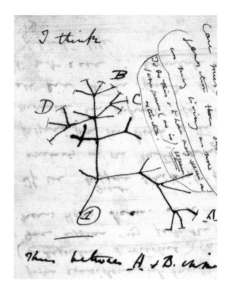

3

This 1953 trademark for Finmar Furniture Limited fuses three elemental forms: tree, human, and letter *F*. Designed by Hans Schleger, the anthropomorphic symbol highlights the linkage between tree and spine. The Ainu people of Japan, for instance, believed that the spine of the first man was made of willow wood.

4

"I think"—so begins English naturalist Charles Darwin's 1837 skeletal diagram of evolutionary relationships. Envisioned as a branching tree, Darwin's theories about common ancestry and the interconnectedness of species would ultimately be published in *On The Origin of Species* in 1859.
DETAIL

5

The contemporary idea of the Christmas tree originated with the Germanic fir of Woden, "on which lights and luminous balls symbolize the sun, moon and stars in the branches of the Cosmic Tree" [Cooper]. Santa Claus hauls a tree, bound for decoration, in this American toy rattle from the 1920s.

6

The Mirrorcube at the Treehotel in Harads, Sweden. Designed by Tham & Videgård Arkitekter in 2010, this treehouse blurs the boundaries between the man-made and the natural. Trees create shelter and carry both maternal and protective significance, which the treehouse magnifies.

FLOWER

The reproductive mechanism of certain plants, the flower is predominantly a symbol of female sexuality and fertility, and hence of life. (From the flower comes the fruit; from the fruit, the seed.) The cup-like form of the flower's calyx is a symbolic vulva, and Chinese poets refer to the vulva as a "lotus." In Hindu tradition the god Brahma emerges from a lotus as if from the womb; the Buddha is birthed by similar means.

The radial flower is inherently solar in its form and can serve as a symbolic proxy for the sun. The heliotropic sunflower tracks the sun's path; the lotus opens with the rising of the sun and closes with its setting, thus representing "solar renaissance" [Cooper] in particular, and rebirth and immortality in general. (See *Sun.*)

The Aztec god of poetry, music, dance, and lust is Xochipilli, or Flower Prince. A 15th-century basalt sculpture of the god depicts him decorated with a variety of hallucinogenic flowers including tobacco, morning glory, and Sinicuichi. He appears to be in a reverie the Aztecs called *temicxoch,* or the flowery dream. The name of the Aztec Flowery War may derive from the belief that, in this warrior-centric culture, an honorable death was beautiful but flower-like in its ephemerality.

The flower has become so commonplace as a visual motif in contemporary culture that it risks becoming drained of any larger meaning. A ubiquitous element of repeating patterns, fabric design, and advertising, the flower telegraphs notions of nature or beauty in a vague but nonetheless appealing manner.

OPPOSITE
Jackie Kennedy on her wedding day, documented by American photographer Toni Frissell on September 12, 1953. The bridal bouquet is dualistic as it signals both purity (e.g. virginity) and fecundity. Paradoxically, a bride's floral wreath has funerary significance in that it marks the "death" of her former life.

2
This Egyptian faience bowl features three rings of lotus petals emanating from a sun-like center. The lotus is a solar and creation symbol that was used in funerary wreaths to suggest rebirth. The repeating wave border reinforces the idea of eternal life. Ptolemaic period, c. 200–150 BCE.

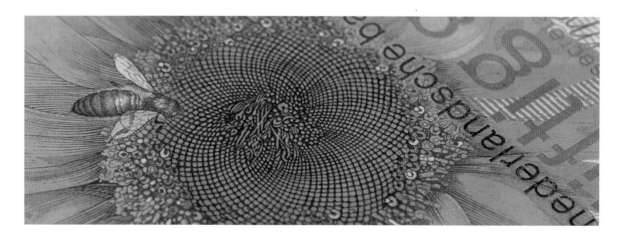

3

Tennessee Williams' *27 Wagons Full of Cotton,* published by New Directions in 1949. A delicate magnolia bloom is violently pinned to rough-hewn wood in a foreshadowing of Flora's sexual assault in the play. Book jacket by American designer Alvin Lustig and photographer J. Connor.

4

Flowers symbolize purity and sacrifice in *Convent Thoughts,* an 1851 painting by British artist Charles Allston Collins. Isolated on a small island of turf within a walled garden, a nun examines a passion flower, a Catholic symbol of Christ's crucifixion. The lily is an emblem of the Virgin Mary that signals the nun's chastity.

5

The 50 gulden banknote created by Dutch designer R.D.E. Oxenaar for De Nederlandsche Bank in 1982. The word *gulden*—guilder in English—means "golden" in Middle Dutch, and Oxenaar's use of a golden sunflower is perhaps a wry reference to the currency's history. DETAIL

6

The cherry blossom is a Japanese symbol of good fortune, but also of evanescence. Fading blooms drift onto a moving raft: the precarious, fleeting moment encapsulates life's transience. *Flower Petals Sprinkling a Raft,* a print by Japanese *ukiyo-e* artist Ando Hiroshige, c. 1848–58.

FRUIT

The (generally) edible container of a tree's seeds, fruit is the equivalent of a hen's egg or woman's womb. It is a protective envelope, certainly, but unlike the shell of an egg—or nut—this enclosure is invitational. The lush colors and sugared scent of ripe fruit make it a traditional symbol of desire and temptation. (See *Egg; Concentric Circles*.)

Fruit's sweetness also seems to be at the heart of its association with pleasure, sexuality, and in Christendom, sin. Tellingly, the Latin word for fruit, *fructus,* is related to the verb *frui,* meaning "to enjoy." William Carlos Williams' 1934 poem "This Is Just To Say," in which the poet describes eating stolen plums in secret, is a deft encapsulation of fruit as a signifier of various kinds of joy.

Fruit is a universal indicator of fertile lands, abundant harvests, and thus prosperity and happiness. The cornucopia—an attribute of the Roman goddesses Ceres and Fortuna—spills over with fruit as a demonstration of nature's plenitude. Fruit is the culmination of processes (or labors) over time: whether for trees or humans, to "bear fruit" is to produce tangible results. Metaphoric fruits include the return on an investment, the end result of an endeavor, or the birth of a child. (See *Horns/Antlers*.)

Specific fruits may have their own cultural associations. As the basis of wine, grapes signified orgiastic initiation to the ancient Greeks, "truth" to the Romans, and blood sacrifice to early Christians. The apple is an Occidental emblem of fertility and love, but its Latin name—*malum*—also means "evil," which may explain the apple's popular identification with the forbidden fruit of Eden. In China and Japan, the peach is apotropaic and represents immortality, while the winter-flowering plum embodies fortitude.

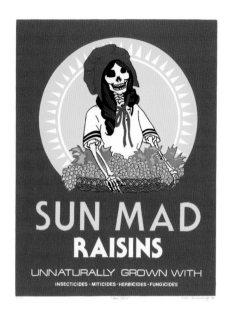

2

OPPOSITE
Still-life painting conventions were established by Dutch and Flemish artists in the 16th and 17th centuries—one of which was the use of fruit to signify ephemerality. Fruit, like the newspaper, has a relatively short life span, and so can serve as a momento mori. *Newspaper and Fruit Dish,* a 1916 still-life painting by Juan Gris.

2
The image of a young woman proffering fruit—a trope of sexuality and fertility—is subverted in this screen print by American artist Ester Hernandez (1982). In a critique of agricultural practices that harm the environment, workers, and consumers, Hernandez exposes the Sun-Maid as a necrotic wraith with toxic grapes.

3

Emerging from the broken jaw of a skull, a serpent grips an apple in this moralizing bronze sculpture from France (c. 1850). The serpent-and-apple is a Christian motif of temptation and sin that references Adam and Eve. The skull—that is, death—may be understood as a figurative piece of fruit, the "yield" of sin.

4

The Japanese decorate their homes in the New Year with a bitter orange known as *daidai*. This citrus is favored because its name is a homophone of the phrase "generation upon generation," a wish for numerous progeny. Japanese woodblock print by Hanzan Matsukawa for the year of the monkey, c. 1860. DETAIL

5

A disembodied orange floats in a black sky like the sun in miniature. Emanating a golden nimbus, this solar orange promises life, rebirth, and immortality—or at least a taste of Southern California sunshine. Sun brand orange crate label, lithography with metallic ink, c. 1930s.

6

Bursting with seeds, the pomegranate is a nearly universal symbol of fertility, abundance, and happiness. The fruit is the basis of auspicious motifs in China, where it signals wishes for hundreds—and even thousands—of sons. China, Jiangxi Province, wheel-thrown porcelain vase with claire-de-lune glaze, 1723–35.

HORSE

BULL

HORNS/ANTLERS

SWINE

COCK

DOG

CAT

APE/MONKEY

LION

TIGER

ELEPHANT

BEAR

FOX

HARE

RAT/MOUSE

BAT

EGG

BIRD

EAGLE

OWL

CROW/RAVEN

BEE

BUTTERFLY

SPIDER

FISH

OCTOPUS

SEASHELL

SNAIL

FROG/TOAD

TORTOISE

SERPENT

HORSE

The wild horse is the embodiment of animal power—speed, strength, virility—and the freedom to express that power. The mustang of the American southwest or the Camargue of the Rhône delta exemplify these qualities, as does the "prancing" black stallion of Italian carmaker Ferrari. Once domesticated, the horse's power can be harnessed—literally—and then channeled: workhorse, draught horse, war-horse.

For millennia the war-horse was a symbol of martial power and conquest: Alexander the Great's war-horse Bucephalus is honored on ancient Greek coins. Marcus Aurelius (Roman), Charlemagne (Carolingian), Philip IV (Spanish), Peter the Great (Russian), and George Washington (American) are all subjects of equestrian statues.

Among the nomads of the central Asian steppes the horse was considered a psychopomp, able to ferry the souls of the dead. Horses were thus commonly sacrificed at the death of their owner and, at times, also buried with them. (Lacking horses, the role of psychopomp was performed by the dog in Aztec and Mayan culture.) (See *Dog.*)

Native Americans first saw the horse via Spanish conquistadores in the 16th century. As the tribes used dogs for portage, the novelty of horses performing this task influenced Native American perceptions of the animal. The Siksika (Blackfoot) named the horse *ponoka-mita,* or elk dog. The Cree knew it as big dog; the Lakota (Sioux) termed the horse *sunkakhan,* or holy dog.

The centaur—half-man, half-horse—is human nature at its most licentious. Greek depictions of Lapiths battling centaurs can be read as an allegory of our internal struggle between measured thought and instinctual urge.

1
The white, winged horse Pegasus is a solar symbol associated with illumination and creative intellect. Rendered in red by American designer Jim Nash in 1933, Mobiloil's trademark emphasizes the fiery aspects of Pegasus' solar symbolism to link it with the internal combustion engine.

2
In the game of chess, the knight's unique manner of movement—an oblique "jump"—is emblematic of the horse as an intuitive animal. German sculptor Josef Hartwig's 1924 chess set features a reductive design in which the L-shaped knight hints at the piece's pattern of movement.

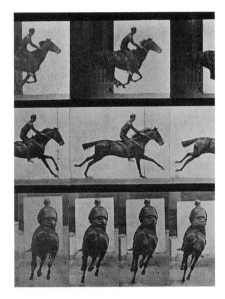

3
The horse and rider can symbolize the Self, the body mastered
by its mind. The horse/rider
relationship can also reflect the
dialectic between instinct and
reason—though if the rational
rider gets lost, it is instinct
that must lead. Plate 633 from
Eadweard Muybridge's *Animal
Locomotion*, 1887. DETAIL

4
This gilt bronze belt plaque
depicts a kneeling horse with two
smaller, inverted horses within
its haunches. What may be a
mare pregnant with foals would
have been a propitious symbol
of fertility and regeneration to
the peoples of the Central Asian
steppes. Chinese, Inner Mongo-
lian, c. 3rd–2nd century BCE.

5
The horse is a marker of hostile
encroachment in this petroglyph
from Canyon del Muerto, or
Canyon of the Dead, Arizona.
Known as the Narbona Panel, the
painting likely records the 1805
Spanish expedition into Diné
(Navajo) territory in which Lt.
Antonio Narbona and his troops
massacred 115 Diné.

6
With its unhinged jaw and vacant
eye sockets, American designer
Gilbert Lesser's iconic horse
head illustration captures the
emotional tone of Peter Schaffer's
1974 psychosexual play *Equus*. The
simultaneous frontal and profile
views evoke the terrified horse
in Pablo Picasso's 1937 painting
Guernica.

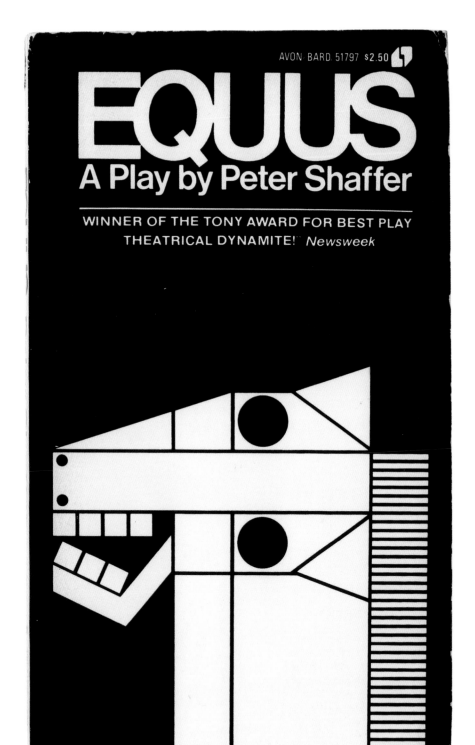

BULL

A nearly universal symbol of solar power, king-ship, and virility, the bull is an attribute of the sun gods Ra (Egyptian) and Baal (Phoenician). The bull's prodigious output of seminal fluid connected it with the fertilizing rain and thus with inseminating sky gods—among them Zeus (Greek), Jupiter (Roman), Indra (Indian), and Thor (Norse). In ancient Persia a primordial bull was believed to be the progenitor of all living things, the earth's plants and animals having been spawned by the bull's blood and semen after its sacrifice by the god Mithras. (See *Sun*.)

Domesticated cattle are ancient markers of wealth, and the Germanic rune known as *feoh, fé,* or *fehu*—approximating the Roman letter *f*—represents the synonymous concepts of cattle and wealth. Indeed, the words cattle and capitalism share the same Latin origin.

Although neutered and therefore impotent, the ox nonetheless represents agrarian fertility when paired with the plough—an implement with phallic significance. In addition, both the bull and ox can evoke (female) fertility when their horns are used as a mnemonic for the lunar crescent. (See *Moon*.)

The aurochs is an extinct species of wild cattle and much of the bull's historical symbolism is likely derived from the imposing presence of the male's sweeping horns. (Its shoulder height approached six feet, and it weighed more than one ton.) To subdue an aurochs would be a notable feat, and Egyptian pharaohs hunted the animal into the Late New Kingdom (c. 1000 BCE) as a confirmation of their supremacy.

1

2

1
The Toraja people revere the water buffalo as a pychopomp that serves to carry the deceased into the afterlife. A human figure framed by bovine horns—as if riding the animal—may depict one such journey. Sulawesi, Indonesia, wooden granary door, 19th to early 20th century.

2
In predynastic Egypt, images of copulating animals were believed to encourage fertility in nature and, by extension, abundance. In *Schwarzer Stier*, German artist Gerhard Marcks emphasizes the bull's reputation for possessing *Zeugungskraft* (fertilizing force). Woodcut, 1922.

3

The bullfight can be understood as a choreographed ritual pitting matador against beast, intellect against brute force, and life against death. That the bull must fulfill its traditional role as a sacrificial animal is a foregone conclusion. Press photograph, Tijuana, Mexico, July 8, 1938.

4

The Roman letter *A* owes its form to earlier glyphs—Egyptian, Cretan, and Phoenician—which depict an ox head with horns. (Inverting the *A* reveals its pictographic origins.) Bell Centennial Bold Listing (1975–78), a typeface by American type designer Matthew Carter.

5

Located at the Palace of Minos at Knossos on Crete, what is thought to be a bull's horns altar is a 20th-century reconstruction by Sir Arthur Evans of the c. 1700–1400 BCE original. Although its intended function and meaning are uncertain, its taurine reference is unambiguous.

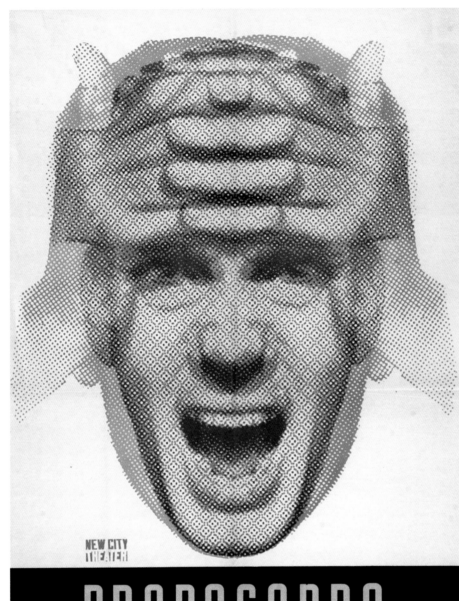

NEW CITY THEATER

PROPAGANDA

PRESENTED BY THE NEW CITY THEATER IN ASSOCIATION WITH
CREATION PRODUCTION CO. / NYC. OPENS SEPTEMBER 8, 1988,
WED. THROUGH SUN. 8PM. TEL. 323-6800. THIS PRODUCTION IS
SUPPORTED, IN PART, BY PONCHO, THE N.E.A., AND THE K.C.A.C.
NEW CITY THEATER / 1634 11TH AVE. / CAPITOL HILL / SEATTLE USA

POSTER DESIGN BY ART CHANTRY

HORNS/ANTLERS

As the animal's head is the seat of its life force, a pair of horns or antlers rising from the head can be understood as emanations or extensions of the animal's vitality. The disembodied horn, therefore, serves as a concentration of animal potency: it represents strength, power, virility, and life itself.

The singular horn, upright, is priapic: a symbol of masculine threat, physical aggression, and sexual power. Inverted and hollowed out, however, the horn becomes a receptacle associated with feminine generative powers, abundance, and feasting. For example, the mythic cornucopia (or Horn of Plenty) is an attribute of the Roman goddesses Ceres and Fortuna; the ritual practice of drinking mead or wine from a horn allows one to symbolically ingest the power of the horn as well as of the animal it represents.

While typically considered male and solar, horns suggest female fertility when their curving form echoes the lunar crescent. The Egyptian goddess Hathor is commonly depicted as a cow with the solar disk cradled in her lunar horns; the mother goddess Isis wears the same crescent moon horns on her headdress. (See *Moon; Bull.*)

In general, the branching antlers of deer are deciduous: they emerge each spring from the head like leafless trees, ultimately toppling in the winter. The annual shedding of antlers thus makes them a symbol of cyclical renewal and rebirth, and of seasonal crop growth. The antlered Celtic god Cernunnos, or The Horned One, is similarly associated with agrarian fertility. (See *Tree; Serpent.*)

2

OPPOSITE
The discombobulating effect of propaganda is suggested by this poster for the New City Theater, created by American designer Art Chantry (1988). Thumbs become horns to signal a man under the sway of the horned god Pan. Like propaganda, Pan is capable of triggering unreasonable fear, or *panic.*

2
Conceived by the 17th-century Japanese shogun Tokugawa Iyeyasu, this family crest is known as *kuwagata,* "helmet horns." Inspired by the shogun's dream, the three interlaced antlers symbolize unity among three leading military clans. The crest was conferred to the Tokugawa clan of Kii.

3

The singular horn is typically phallic, but its emergence from the forehead of the unicorn dilutes its erotic significance and transforms it into a symbol of intellect and reason (when it is not symbolizing rarity or, more often, wishful thinking). Valued for its magical properties during the Renaissance, unicorn horn—or *alicorn*—was widely believed to purify water and treat disease. The illusory nature of the mythical beast is evoked in this illustration by Spanish designer Javier Jaén for the *New York Times Magazine* (2015).

4
"Greetings from Krampus." An Austro-Hungarian invention, Krampus is the malefic companion of St. Nicholas who frightens ill-behaved children and, when necessary, beats them with his birch-rod. Krampus' horns link him with the satanic on this early 20th-century Hungarian Christmas postcard.

5
A portrait of the Apsaroke (or Crow) elder Bull Chief by American photographer Edward S. Curtis, c. 1908. To the Plains Indians, the buffalo was a symbol of supernatural power, fortitude, and plenitude. Bull Chief's horned headdress imbues him with the qualities of a bison bull.

6
Ram horns are an attribute of the Greco-Egyptian god Zeus Ammon, a favorite of Alexander the Great. In an effort to "deify" Alexander after his death, curving horns were added to his portrait—as well as to those of his warhorse Bucephalus. Thracian silver tetradrachm, 323–281 BCE.

7
Traditionally used to announce, alert, or summon, the sounding of the horn represents the role of advertising in this trademark for the Andrew Coyne Agency by American designer Clarence P. Hornung (c. 1930). The *shofar* is a ram's-horn trumpet still blown during Jewish religious observances.

SWINE

Ancient pantheistic cultures tend to view swine more favorably than those that developed under the sway of monotheism. In Egyptian, Greek, Celtic, and Sino-Vietnamese thought, the sow is a symbol of maternal care, female fecundity, plenitude, and thus wealth and luck. The Egyptian sky goddess Nut is depicted as a celestial sow tending to her innumerable progeny—the stars—and so Egyptian women wore pig amulets to court fertility and good fortune. The sow was associated with the Great Mother in Mesopotamia and pre-Hellenic Greece, and possessed lunar and fertility significance for the Celts. (See *Moon.*)

Aggressive and intrepid in battle, the wild boar was a favored motif among Mycenaean, Roman, Persian, Norse, and Japanese warriors. The boar was especially venerated by the Celts who believed it had apotropaic powers; its meat was eaten by warriors and priests at sacred feasts. Pork was also buried with slain warriors to sustain them on their journey to the afterlife.

Conversely, Judaism and Islam consider the pig an unclean animal and so forbid the eating of pork. That the Christ would exorcise demons only to let them possess a herd of swine exemplifies the low regard with which the animal is held in Christendom. Wallowing in filth, the domesticated pig has become—in much of the Occident—a symbol of indolence, ignorance, and by extension, moral corruption. Its seemingly insatiable appetite and indiscriminate eating habits also contribute to its reputation for gluttony and lust; that the sow is capable of cannibalizing her farrow only reinforces these associations.

1

1
German artist George Grosz—who once noted that "all men are pigs"—reimagines the Greek myth of Circe in the context of the decadent Weimar Republic. A bourgeois pig and a prostitute kiss: their tongues touching, the beast's open mouth and teeth signal his avarice. *Circe,* watercolor, 1927.

2

The pig is so central to Chinese conceptions of domestic well-being that the word for home (*jia*) is written by placing the pig character under the symbol for roof. (A home without a pig is consequently no home at all.) Contemporary cut-paper design to mark the Chinese zodiac sign.

3

A scene from the film *Carrie*, by American director Brian De Palma (1976). Although blood is generally a symbol of vitality and life-force, the blood of a pig—an "unclean" animal—is a symbolic contaminant. Prom queen Carrie White is publicly humiliated with a shower of pig's blood in a cruel allusion to her first menstruation.

4

Associated with winter solstice feasts, the boar's head is a traditional European symbol of life force and good fortune. Present-day Germans still celebrate the new year by exchanging a candy *Glucksschwein*, or lucky pig. An *M* and *W* trademark for the firm of Mette & Wrede by German designer Karl Schulpig, 1922.

5

Two ancient British silver coins minted by Celtic tribes around the 1st century CE: the Iceni (*left*), and the Corieltavi (*right*). Both coins feature a stylized boar whose distinguishing feature is its erect dorsal bristles. Celtic warriors spiked and stiffened their hair with lime to mimic the boar's fearsome appearance in battle.

COCK

As the herald and avatar of the sunrise, the cockerel is associated with the solar cycle and hence with renewal and rebirth. To the ancient Greeks the bird evoked Persephone's return from the netherworld each spring; to early Christians the cock signified the resurrection of Jesus and the triumph of light (i.e. righteousness) over darkness. (See *Sun; Bee.*)

In ancient Egypt, Greece, and Rome, the rooster—patiently awaiting the dawn—symbolized vigilance and prescience. Its later use on the roofs of European clock towers and churches is predicated on these apotropaic powers: "the gilded, solar cock guards the steeple through the hours of darkness when the bells are silent" [Cooper].

The bird's virility make it a durable symbol of male sexuality, and its onomatopoetic English name, *cock,* is a common slang term for the phallus. (The derivative adjectives cocksure and cocky conjure the brash, strutting disposition of both young men and the territorial bird.) In related symbolism, Tibetan Buddhism locates the cock at the center of the Wheel of Life as the embodiment of lust and attachment to the material world.

Aggressive and pugilistic, the rooster is sacred to Ares, the Greek god of war, and was depicted on the shields of Greek hoplites to convey their eagerness for battle. The word cockpit, now used to describe the cabin of an airplane or racing car, originally described the pit or enclosure used for staging cockfights.

The cock's color may be a cue to its symbolism: red suggests (solar) fire; the golden cock is the dawn. Black is malefic; in Chinese tradition the white cock offers protection from ghosts.

1

1
The cockfight can typify humanity's struggles against adversity, and depictions of gamecocks on Roman sarcophagi may be religious allegories "of the soul's ultimate victory over death and darkness" [Shepherd]. Two birds in "a hotel for fighting cocks," photographed in Puerto Rico by Edwin Rosskam, 1937.

2
Designed by Helmut Müller-Molo, this poster advertises a 1935 Dresden exhibition of firefighting and rescue. *Der Rote Hahn* illustrates a colloquial German expression: to put the "red rooster" on someone's roof is to set it on fire. Given the firebombing of Dresden a decade later, this poster is eerily prescient.

3

This terracotta cockerel, marked with the letters of the Etruscan alphabet, is believed to be an inkwell. The act of lifting the stopper opens the bird's beak, prompting the cock to figuratively crow: heralding a new day becomes analogous to heralding a new (written) thought. The radiating motif inscribed on the stopper augments the solar symbolism of the crenellated comb. Etruscan, c. 650–600 BCE.

4

German designer Karl Schulpig uses a screeching rooster to promote the services of Berlin poster printer Dinse & Eckert (1921). This avian alarm is an apt metaphor for the medium of the poster, a form of publicity that Italian adman Dino Villani once described as a "paper siren."

5

A contemporary weathercock on the roof of a house in Somerset, England. As an ancient symbol of vigilance, the cock is commonly incorporated into weather vanes to guard against evil. The spinning vane allows the cock to scan the landscape in each of the cardinal directions.

DOG

The symbolism of the dog is ambivalent, and depends on whether the animal is domesticated or wild, leashed or free. Indeed, the family dog is *Canis familiaris;* its untamed antecedent, the grey wolf, is *Canis lupus.*

Known in the Occident as "man's best friend," the dog is a traditional symbol of loyalty and marital fidelity. (The colloquial name for a pet dog, *Fido,* is Latin for "I trust.") This notion of faithful companionship during life extended even beyond death, and European medieval sarcophagi commonly feature a dog at the foot of its master. In Aztec and Mayan mythology, dogs were believed to serve as psychopomps at death, safely guiding souls on their journey through the underworld.

Watchdogs embody vigilance and can possess otherworldly powers of detection. To the Tabwa people of Zaire, dogs have *malosi,* a vision that allows them to see "the odious activities of witches and sorcerers invisible to ordinary eyes" [Roberts]. Other cultures believed that dogs were able to "see" ghosts.

In Jewish and Islamic thought, dogs are unclean animals, associated with gluttony and lust. (A 2014 Malaysian event, "I Want to Touch a Dog," prompted fury from Islamic fundamentalists.) To be called a "dog" is an insult in most quarters; "imperialist running dogs" was an epithet favored by communist China in the 1950s.

To leash a dog is to curb its animal nature; to unleash it is to invite unpredictability. In Shakespeare's *Julius Caesar,* when Mark Antony exclaims, "Cry 'Havoc,' and let slip the dogs of war," he summons the chaos of untethered dogs.

2

OPPOSITE
A portrait of musician Beck by American artist Greg Clarke in the year that "Odelay" was released (1996). Clarke depicts Beck as an innocent young pup, albeit one with sideburns and stubble. The English word puppy derives from the French *poupée,* meaning doll or toy.

2
Cerberus, the three-headed sentinel of Greek and Roman mythology, in a trademark by German designer Max Hertwig (c. 1924–30). Hertwig envisions Cerberus as a fire-breathing beast with an almost machined form, an appropriate symbol for a manufacturer of industrial coal-fired furnaces.

3
A family dog reclines on a love seat in this 2¾ × 3¼-inch daguerreotype, c. 1855. The preciousness of the image is underscored by its small size, cost, and the reverence with which it is presented. This style of portrait is most often reserved for lovers, spouses, children, or other intimates.

4
An impression of a baked clay *sello*, or seal, from pre-Columbian Veracruz, made by Jorge Enciso in the 1940s. In ancient Mexico dogs were sacrificed and buried alongside the dead to provide companionship and to serve as spirit guides to the underworld.

5
A leashed dog is a symbol of order, a reassuring sign of human control over an unpredictable nature. A Basenji accompanies his master in the afterlife on this limestone Egyptian tomb relief. The hunting dog's name, indicated by the hieroglyphs above him, is *hbn*, or ebony. 2435–2152 BCE. DETAIL

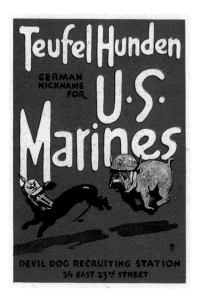

6

Teufel Hunden, a WWI recruitment poster attributed to American illustrator Charles B. Falls. Intended as an insult by opposing German forces, the term Devil Dogs is now an honorific among US Marines who have a reputation for dogged determination.

7

Invented by Japanese artist Hajime Sorayama and released by Sony Corporation in 1999, Aibo is an "entertainment robot" in the guise of a dog. (*Aibo* means companion.) Sixty years before Aibo, Westinghouse Electric displayed its own robot dog, Sparko, at the 1939 World's Fair.

8

A 20th-century metal sign with a timeless message. *Cave Canem,* or Beware of Dog, is a common motif in Roman threshold mosaics from the 1st century BCE. As guardians, dogs are often positioned at points of entry and exit, such as doorways and borders.

9

The Japanese folk toy *Inu hariko,* or papier-mâché dog, on a stamp issued in 1958. *Inu hariko* has apotropaic powers, protecting children and women during childbirth. During the Edo period (1603–1868), it was "customary to write the kanji character for dog (*inu*) on the forehead of children" [Frédéric] to keep them safe.

CAT

The dog is a symbol of loyalty and obedience, but the domesticated cat—independent, self-reliant— epitomizes freedom. The cat's transience is inextricably tied to its sexual liberty, a linkage noted by Japanese poet Issa in this haiku from 1818:

> *From darkness*
> *to darkness,*
> *the loves of a cat.*

The nocturnal black cat, a tomcat, was the namesake of *Le Chat Noir,* the notorious 19th-century Montmartre cabaret that embodied freedom from bourgeois constraints. To "cat" or "cat around" is late-18th-century British slang for the search for a sexual partner.

Generally lunar and *yin,* the cat is a traditional attribute of female deities, among them Bast (Egyptian), Artemis (Greek), and Feyja (Scandinavian). The cat-headed moon goddess Bast represented fertility, motherhood, and protection; as Bast's cult animal, the cat was identified with both the moon and pregnant women. The variable appearance of a cat's eyes was also likened to the changing appearance of the moon. (See *Moon.*)

Medieval Europe viewed the cat as a witch's familiar—her diabolical assistant—or even as a witch incarnate. ("Hellcat" is a 17th-century English synonym for witch.) In symbolic exorcisms, cats were burned alive in bonfires across Europe as part of Christian feast day celebrations. For more than 400 years the French city of Metz burned cats on "Cat Wednesday" during Lent; the Belgian city of Ypres celebrated the same day by throwing cats from the Cloth Hall tower to the square below.

1

2

1
Believed to shift between feline and female form, the cat is a symbol of transformation. This 1932 photographic self-portrait by Italian Futurist Wanda Wulz, *Io + gatto,* captures what appears to be just such a metamorphosis—although whether from cat to woman or from woman to cat is unclear.

2
The Cat's Paw Rubber Company harnesses the cat's reputation for sure-footedness on this 1941 package by German designer Lucian Bernhard. That the cat is black is unremarkable in contemporary culture; to medieval eyes, it would have signified misfortune, evil, and death.

3

In Tennessee Williams' 1955 play *Cat on a Hot Tin Roof,* Maggie "the cat" is a figure of unfulfilled sexual desire. Like the cat who is able to leap from a roof and land uninjured, Maggie is a symbol of cunning and survival. Dust jacket by American designer Alvin Lustig for New Directions.

4

The *maneki-neko,* or beckoning cat, is a symbol of good fortune in Japan, where it is placed in shop windows to attract customers (and prosperity). Although its origins are unclear, the beckoning cat was a symbol of the Japanese demimonde during the Meiji era. In the earlier Edo period, geisha were sometimes called *neko* (cat), and Meiji depictions of geisha show the women "beckoning" customers for business with the same gesture as the talismanic cat. Japan, early 20th century, painted clay.

5

The ancient Egyptian word for cat is *miu,* an onomatopoeic name derived from the cat's meow. (Contemporary Arabic uses the word *mau.*) The cat hieroglyph represents the sound *miu,* and is combined with other glyphs to form the text on this wall at the Temple of Hathor, Dendera, Egypt, c. 51–30 BCE.

APE/MONKEY

Perceptive, inquisitive, and agile, the monkey would be the pinnacle of animal intelligence were it not for its close relation, *Homo sapiens.* Almost human—but not quite—the monkey serves as a reminder of our own unruly and infantile nature.

Buddhism identifies the monkey as one of the Three Senseless Creatures, an emblem of greed. Its "monkey mind" is fickle, distractible, and undisciplined—an allegory of humans in thrall with the material world. "To ape" is to mindlessly imitate, and French painter Jean-Baptiste-Siméon Chardin's 1740 canvas *The Monkey Painter* seems as much a critique of simian tendencies as of still-life painters.

In the Occident the ape can symbolize brutal, bestial tendencies, and a number of wartime propaganda posters depict the enemy—whether Hun or Bolshevik—as a hairy beast on a murderous rampage. (One classic example: the 1917 US Army enlistment poster *Destroy This Mad Brute,* by H.R. Hopps.) Traditional Christian iconography uses the ape as a symbol of lechery or as an incarnation of Satan. *Simia Dei,* or Ape of God, was an epithet for the devil in the Middle Ages.

Egypt, India, Mesoamerica, and Japan are regions that have historically looked more favorably on the monkey. As the incarnation of the god Thoth, the baboon was a symbol of wisdom and a patron of the scribal arts in ancient Egypt. A degree of wisdom is suggested by the 17th-century carving of the Three Monkeys at the Toshogu Shrine in Nikko, Japan. With eyes, ears, and mouth covered, the monkeys illustrate restraint and discipline, the antithesis of "monkey mind."

OPPOSITE
This ivory *netsuke* is a succinct encapsulation of *Sanbiki no saru,* the Three Monkeys who see, hear, and speak no evil. In Japanese, the word "monkey" (*saru*) and the verb-ending "not" (*-zaru*) are homophonic; this *netsuke* may be a mnemonic to refrain from evil. Carved by Masatsugu Kaigyokusai in the 19th century.

2
The monkey is a favored comic stand-in for artists and writers. American designer Michael Schwab created this literate monkey as a trademark for humorist David Sedaris in 2010. German designer Emil Preetorius explored a similar motif—minus the reading glasses—in an ex libris for Hans and Milly Witt, c. 1910.

3   4

5

3

A Dogon mask representing *Dege*, or the Black Monkey. In mourning ceremonies following the death of a Dogon male, the dancer wearing this mask is purposely lewd and inappropriate, exemplifying "the ugly male from the bush" [Vogel and N'Diaye] who is not to be emulated. Mali, wood, c. mid-20th century.

4

Hanuman, the Hindu monkey god, symbolizes benevolence and fealty because of his absolute devotion to Rama. Contemporary India still reveres the monkey as Hanuman's representative; following tradition, Hindus feed feral monkeys twice a week. India, gouache on paper, c. 1870.

5

A monkey faces the sun in this repeating pattern from a cylindrical stamp from pre-Columbian Mexico. The monkey, or *ozomatli,* was the companion and servant of Flower Prince, the Aztec god of poetry, music, dance, and lust. Those born under the day sign of the monkey were thought to be adept at the arts.

6

British scientist Charles Darwin and his theory of evolution are mercilessly lampooned in this illustration from *The Hornet* in 1871. (The caricature was prompted by the then-recent publication of Darwin's *The Descent of Man.*) In this context, the deëvolution of Darwin—half man, half beast—is shorthand for quack science.

A VENERABLE ORANG-OUTANG.

A CONTRIBUTION TO UNNATURAL HISTORY.

LION

The male lion is a bestial monarch. Golden in color, its face framed by a corona-like mane, the lion is associated with the blinding light and fiery heat of the noonday sun. As a symbol of strength and majesty, the lion's role in the Occident corresponds to that of the tiger in Asia, and to the eagle in general. (See *Nimbus; Sun; Tiger; Eagle.*)

The negative symbolism of the lion's power, however, remains ever-present. When opened, its disquieting jaws have the effect of an eclipse: the lion immediately "ceases to be bright and solar and becomes dark and chthonian" [Chevalier & Gheerbrant]. An attribute of war gods, the lion is a symbol of war's carnage and can embody ruthlessness and cruelty. As an emblem of monarchs and empires it can represent arrogant or capricious rule. (See *Mouth/Tongue.*)

The lioness accompanies mother fertility goddesses and virginal warrior goddesses, among them Cybele (Phrygian), Artemis (Greek), Fortuna (Roman), and Tara (Indian). In general, the lioness simultaneously evokes the tender side of maternal care, as well as its more fearsome protective aspects. The avenging leonine goddess Sekhmet—known as the flaming eye of Ra—proved so zealous at killing that the ancient Egyptians did their best to keep her impaired with offerings of beer.

The lion is often paired with other animals to form political or mythical allegories. The lion and unicorn, symbols of the United Kingdom, are oppositional but complementary: England and Scotland, solar and lunar, male and female. The lion's killing of the boar represents the sun's annual triumph over the winter. Based on a Biblical prophecy, the image of the lion and lamb living in harmony is a symbol of paradise on earth.

2

OPPOSITE
A lone horse falls prey to a ravening lion at the mouth of a cave. When emblematic of death, the typically golden lion may appear infernal, reflecting latent qualities echoed by the landscape of this painting. *A Lion Attacking a Horse,* by British painter George Stubbs. Oil on canvas, 1770.
DETAIL

2
Narasimha, the human-feline incarnation of the Hindu god Vishnu. Literally "man-lion," Narasimha is a fluid response to dualistic thought. Vishnu assumes this form—neither fully man nor beast—to kill a demon without violating the terms of a divine edict. India, brass mask, c. 18th century.

3

The lion is a traditional symbol of vigilance and protection in Asia, where it is believed to ward off evil. The large cat is foreign to Japan, however, and so its depiction can range from the fanciful to the comic. Known as *karashishi*, or "dog of Buddha," this lion *netsuke* has apotropaic significance. Ivory, possibly 18th century.

4

A roaring lion—the heraldic charge of Henry the Lion, Duke of Saxony—has symbolized the German city of Braunschweig since the duke installed a bronze lion outside his residence in the 12th century. Swiss designer Hermann Eidenbenz created this version of the *Burglöwe* (castle lion) more than 750 years later.

5

Although the lion is a royal animal in Africa, it can represent predation and cruelty. Glélé, the 19th-century "lion king" of Dahomey, was a notorious slave profiteer whose reign entailed human sacrifice. Fon people, Republic of Benin, brass and copper, 20th century.

6

The lion and its fiery mane appear decidedly solar on this late medieval ceiling tile known as a *socarrat*. Positioned to look down from between ceiling crossbeams, the leonine sun is an icon of terrestrial and celestial power. Spain, possibly Paterna, earthenware with glaze and black paint, 1490–1550.

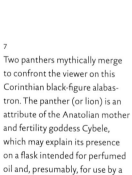

7
Two panthers mythically merge to confront the viewer on this Corinthian black-figure alabastron. The panther (or lion) is an attribute of the Anatolian mother and fertility goddess Cybele, which may explain its presence on a flask intended for perfumed oil and, presumably, for use by a woman. In an odd coincidence, the later Christian text *Physiologus* asserts that a "sweet fragrance" emanates from the panther's voice. Greece, terracotta, 640–625 BCE.

8
The Lion of Venice keeping watch over the Piazza San Marco in Venice, Italy. The winged lion is an early Christian symbol of the apostle Mark, patron saint of the city. The lion and eagle hybrid— comprised of two "kings"—suggests dominance over earth and sky. Cilicia, bronze, with the body dating from c. 400–300 BCE.

9
The Cowardly Lion in filmmaker Victor Fleming's 1939 musical *The Wizard of Oz*. Based on a character created by author L. Frank Baum, the Cowardly Lion is full of bluster—he frightens others with his "terrible roar"—but he is ultimately ineffectual. Rather than personifying courage, he embodies impotence.

TIGER

In general, the tiger's role in Asia is analogous to that of the lion's in the Occident: both cats tend to be considered solar, celestial, omnipotent, and *yang.* In India and Japan the tiger is an attribute of gods and warriors; in China it is an emblem of courage and authority associated with military valor. It is also royal, a king among beasts: the pattern of stripes on the tiger's forehead is generally "read" as the Chinese character *wang,* meaning king. (See *Lion; Sun.*)

Feared even by demons, the tiger was thought capable of dispelling evil in ancient China, and tiger effigies were stationed near residential doorways and in graveyards to offer protection to both the living and the dead. The fifth day of the fifth moon was considered especially inauspicious; on this day Chinese parents would write the "three-striped" character *wang* on their children's foreheads, marking their young with the protective sign of the tiger.

The cat's ability to navigate and hunt in low-lighting conditions—its night vision is approximately six times better than our own—links the tiger with uncommon powers of perception and suggest an "inner light" [Matthews]. The title of *The Tiger's Eye,* an avant-garde art and literature quarterly published in America from 1947 to 1949, suggests related symbolism. (See *Eagle; Owl.*)

The tiger's negative connotations stem from its wild nature, in particular its unpredictability and ferocity. The Hindu god Shiva is commonly depicted sitting on a tiger skin to indicate that "he has subdued the unbridled passions to which others are prey" [Shepherd]. For Buddhists, the tiger is one of the "senseless creatures," an emblem of irrational anger.

1

1

One-stroke Tiger, a hanging scroll over five feet in length by Chinese scholar and imperial tutor Weng Tonghe. Written in the lunar year of the tiger in 1902, the character *hu* (or tiger) represents the date, the animal and its talismanic powers, and likely Weng himself, as he was born under the sign of the tiger. Contrasting this character with one Weng wrote twelve years earlier is intriguing: his brush thick with ink, the tiger of 1890 is deft and bold, but required three strokes. The later *One-stroke Tiger*—written when Weng was 72—appears lean by comparison, but this feline is more shrewd. Ink on red paper.

8　　　　　　　　　　　　　　　9

2

In an allegory of Indian resistance to British colonialism, a native tiger mauls a prostrate foreigner. Known as "Tippoo's Tiger," this mechanical organ was made for Tipu Sultan, the self-styled "Tiger of Mysore" who ruled over that kingdom in southern India until 1799. Painted wood and metal, c. 1793.

3

This Ottoman fritware tile features a pattern of alternating tiger stripes and leopard spots, thereby transforming the ceramic into a symbolic pelt. Although its exact meaning is uncertain, the stripes-and-spots motif may have held apotropaic significance: in China, for example, tigers are believed to ward off evil and so small boys wear hats and shoes decorated with tiger motifs; in ancient Egypt the leopard's spots were likened to eyes, and so came to represent vigilance. Syria, Damascus, c. 1550–1600.

4

The nose art of these Curtis P-40 Warhawks identifies them as belonging to the "Flying Tigers," a squadron of volunteer American fighter pilots operating in Southeast Asia in 1941 and 1942. Aptly named, the Tigers displayed indomitable courage in their defense of China against Japanese aggression.

ELEPHANT

The world's largest terrestrial mammal, the elephant is an imposing animal with no predators—other than man—that has long embodied fortitude and power. A symbol of kingship and sovereignty, the elephant is included in Indian, Chinese, and Arabic games of chess due to its historical role in warfare. War elephants fought in the armies of ancient India, Persia, and Greece; the Carthaginian general Hannibal crossed the Alps with elephants in 218 BCE during the Second Punic War.

With its massive, columnar legs the elephant evokes concepts of permanence and stability—which may explain its role in Indian and Tibetan folklore as a kind of Atlas supporting the cosmos on its back. Giovanni Bernini's elephant bearing an obelisk in Rome (1667) and the Carlsberg brewery's Elephant Gate in Copenhagen (1901) exemplify the use of the pachyderm as an architectural caryatid. (See *Tortoise*.)

Admired for its intelligence and excellent memory, the elephant symbolizes wise rule and good governance, especially in Africa and India. That an elephant can live seventy years only enhances its reputation for sagacity.

The word "elephant," from the Greek *elephas*, means ivory, and the animal's significance is inextricably linked to its tusks. (The ivory trade was a fixture of colonial Africa for more than a century, so much so that one West African nation is still known as Côte d'Ivoire, or Ivory Coast.) With populations in decline throughout the world, the elephant's "value" needs to be decoupled from ivory if the animal is to survive in the wild.

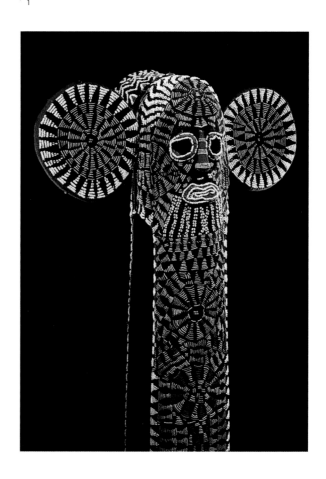

1

1
Symbol of the authority to govern, an elaborately beaded Kuosi society elephant mask can only be worn by the Bamileke *fon* (king) and fellow secret society members. Glass beads—formerly used by the Bamileke as currency—enhance the mask's use as a marker of prestige. Cameroon, 20th century.

3

4

2
Ganesha is the elephant-headed Hindu god of wisdom and writing who snapped off one of his own tusks to transcribe the epic poem *Mahabharata* when his pen failed. A carved and painted effigy of Ganesha looks out from his niche at the Vaital Deul temple in Bhubaneswar, India. Late 8th or 9th century.

3
This calcite amulet evokes an elephant's head with minimal cues: two eyes, a pair of curving tusks, and a stout trunk. While its significance is unclear, the ability to symbolically hold an elephant in the palm of one's hand would have conferred great power to the amulet's owner. Egypt, Predynastic Period, c. 4000–3200 BCE.

4
Hunting-as-sport is a privilege of the wealthy that serves to affirm their rank. American President Theodore Roosevelt displays his mastery over the natural world— embodied by the dead elephant on which he leans—on an African safari around 1909. Glass lantern slide by Edward Van Altena.

BEAR

Easily shifting from a quadrupedal to bipedal stance, the bear can be seen as a kind of proto-human, albeit one with superhuman powers. The Ainu of Northern Japan worshipped the bear as a mountain god and understood it to be the pro-genitor of their race; similar beliefs were shared by Siberian tribes in the Amur River basin, as well as by some Native Americans. The Algonquin Indi-ans, for instance, called the bear "Grandfather."

In Northern Europe and parts of Asia it was con-sidered taboo to utter the bear's "true" name lest it somehow summon the fearsome beast. (The Soyots of Siberia believed that the earth itself served as the bear's ears.) As a result a number of euphemisms emerged, among them the Slavic *medved* (honey-eater) and the English bear, Dutch *bruin,* and Old Norse *björn,* all of which mean brown. Wary Siberian hunters referred to the bear as "Old Fellow" or "Lord of the Forest."

Retiring underground for months, the bear's practice of winter hibernation made it a symbol of the moon's phases among the ancient Greeks and Celts. (The animal was sacred to the lunar goddesses Artemis and Diana.) Like the cyclic appearance of the moon, the bear's return in the spring suggests regeneration and resurrection. (See *Moon.*)

Belief in the protective and transformative pow-ers of the bear—and by extension, its pelt—was pervasive. During rituals dedicated to Artemis, young Athenian girls known as *arktoi* or she-bears shed ceremonial bearskins to mark their maturation into women. Viking warriors known as *berserkers*—literally bear-shirted—dressed in bear pelts (and may have ingested stimulants) to trigger their metamorphosis into fearless, ursine-like fighters.

1

1
A sea bear—half-grizzly bear, half-killer whale—is depicted in this late-19th-century Haida mask. As the rulers of their respective realms, the grizzly and orca were venerated by peoples on the Northwest Coast of America. Both animals were believed to be capable of taking a human form, thus embodying the idea of trans-formation. Ritually wearing this mask would have enabled the initiate to undergo a similar metamorphosis: from human to mythic sea bear, and back. Canada, British Columbia; beaten copper, inlaid shell, sea-otter fur.

2

A 50 pfennig banknote with a heraldic bear, rampant, issued by the German city of Berlin. The bear—often upright—has personified Berlin since the early 13th century. That it no longer wears a neck collar is an indication that the bear (and thus Berlin) is "free" and not subject to imperial rule. *Notgeld*, 1921.

3

A mother bear shelters her cub in this proposed trademark for the California Conservation Corps. The California grizzly and cub represent the CCC's fierce commitment to safeguarding California's future—its natural resources. By American designer Michael Vanderbyl, 1978.

4

This luster-painted fritware plate from Kashan, Iran, features a spotted bear strolling through the night. Although the meaning of the 12th-century design is uncertain, it may playfully allude to the constellation *Al Dubb al Akbar*—the Greater Bear—in which case the spots may be read as stars.

FOX

Noted for its intelligence and elusiveness, the fox symbolizes nimbleness and cunning at its best, hypocrisy and deceit at its worst. (As verbs, "to fox" is to trick through ingenuity; "to outfox" is to outwit.) This reputation for wiliness can engender begrudging respect or outright scorn.

In the Orient the fox is mythically associated with longevity, seduction, and virility. After living for one thousand years, the fox becomes nine-tailed and assumes even greater powers of seduction. (In Chinese numerology the number nine is auspicious because *nine* and *longevity* are homonyms.) In Japanese folklore the fox (*kitsune*) is a shapeshifter who can take the form of a monk or, more commonly, an attractive young woman. These "fox-women" bewitch and seduce unsuspecting men, and embody unbridled sexual desire.

In a more prosaic role, the fox is also an attribute of the Japanese rice god Inari. As grain-destroying rodents are one of its main food sources, the fox is seen as a protector of the rice crop; pairs of white votive foxes are common features at shrines throughout Japan.

In Christian tradition the red fox's coloration was linked to fire and thus to the infernal. Coupled with its reputation for trickery, the red fox came to represent Satan, the predator of souls who uses guile to entrap his prey. The fox's bushy tail is another of its distinguishing features, and is the basis of its name in English. *Fox,* German *fuchs*—both stem from the Sanskrit *puccha,* meaning tail. With their tails of trailing light, shooting stars are known colloquially in Japan as "sky foxes."

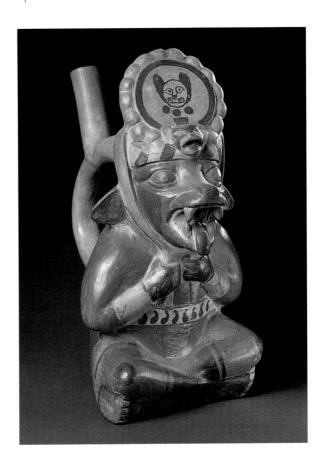

1

1
This Moche ceramic depicts a fox-headed human wearing the "ritual runner" headdress associated with warrior-priests. It is thought that Moche priests ingested San Pedro cactus—which contains the hallucinogen mescaline—in order to enter altered states of consciousness. In this context the fox may serve as a symbol of that psychotropic transformation. Stirrup-spout vessel, Peru, c. 400–700 CE.

2

A recurring character in the moral tales of Aesop, the fox is a trickster in "The Fox and the Stork" and a keen judge of character in "The Fox and the Mask." In the fable of "The Fox and the Goat," the fox embodies blatant opportunism. Linocut by Danish illustrator Simon Væth, 2010.

3

This photograph of American debutante Louise Cromwell was likely taken in 1911, prior to her first marriage. With a white fox pelt draped around her neck and another coiled in her lap, Cromwell appears as an urbane Artemis, the virginal huntress of Greek mythology.

4

In traditional Japanese Noh theater the *kitsune* mask can typify a female vulpine spirit who is seductive—and dangerous. In contemporary Mandarin, *huli jin* (or fox-spirit) remains a derogatory term for a beguiling woman. *Netsuke* signed by Takashige, boxwood, 19th century.

5

A still from American director Wes Anderson's stop-motion animated film *Fantastic Mr. Fox* (2009). Based on the book by Roald Dahl, the film pits an intelligent fox against three rich but nasty farmers. Mr. Fox represents the bon vivant who prefers thievery to honest work.

HARE

The hare (or rabbit) is a universal symbol of fertility. Viewed positively, this attribute affirms life and its renewal; viewed negatively, as in Christian traditions, it is equated with sexual impropriety and wantonness. (The Playboy bunny icon, designed by art director Art Paul in 1953, celebrates the hare's propensity for mating.)

Nocturnal and considered a lunar animal, the hare is so closely identified with the earth's only natural satellite that it can symbolize the moon by proxy. The moon's associations with rebirth, resurrection, and immortality are thus easily shared by the hare. In Chinese folklore, the Jade Rabbit mixes the elixir of immortality on the moon with a mortar and pestle. (See *Moon*.)

The hare is notoriously skittish and can signify cowardice. It can also play the role of the trickster, however, using its cunning (and speed) to outwit larger and stronger foes. West African and Native American oral traditions form the basis of the character Br'er Rabbit in the *Uncle Remus* stories (1881); Warner Bros.' Bugs Bunny is a modern incarnation of the trickster hare.

In Teutonic and Anglo-Saxon myth the hare symbolizes dawn and inception. The hare-headed moon goddess Oestra (or Eostre) appears to have lent her name to the words "east" (origin of the rising sun) and "Easter" (the spring festival). Oestra is accompanied by a hare—now known as the Easter bunny—who lays eggs at the time of the spring equinox. Eggs reinforce the hare's fertility and life symbolism while effectively neutralizing its mammalian sexual overtones. (See *Egg*.)

1
In Japanese lore the hare offers itself as a meal to the hungry Buddha by leaping onto a fire; in return, Buddha honors the hare's selflessness by affixing its image to the moon. This 19th-century Japanese *netsuke* signed by Anrakusai evokes the folktale in miniature form.

2
This 1928 American trademark features four hares in a cyclical motif that suggests eternity and immortality. The 6th-century Chinese prototype, a triskele with three hares whose shared ears form a triangle, is the model for versions used in medieval European churches, where it symbolizes the Trinity.

3

A Mimbre black-on-white painted bowl depicts a rabbit astride the crescent moon, about 750–1100 CE. The later Aztec Codex Borgia includes a glyph of a rabbit sitting in a U-shaped crescent moon that likely alludes to the womb—and so to the rabbit's fertility.

4

American artist Gary Baseman's vinyl toy *Dumb Luck* (1999) embodies the meaning of the term "harebrained." The European Iron Age practice of using the hare's foot as a symbol of good luck may ultimately derive from its phallic form.

5

The hare's reputation for prolific reproduction make it a natural symbol of sexual fervor. The Vibratex Rabbit Habit erotic toy features a vibrating bunny with quivering ears. DETAIL

6

To be "as mad as a March hare" is to exhibit lunacy. This usually timid animal seems to behave oddly during the spring breeding season, running erratically and "boxing" with its mates. Illustration of the March Hare and Mad Hatter by John Tenniel in Lewis Carroll's *Alice's Adventures in Wonderland*, 1865.

RAT/MOUSE

The words "rat" and "rodent" both stem from the Latin *rodere,* meaning "to gnaw." While this impulse is generally seen as a sign of the rat's avarice and destructiveness, in India the rat's incessant nibbling is considered "a metaphor for the acquisition of knowledge" [Shepherd]. In some Renaissance paintings the motif of a black and white rat symbolizes night and day, eating away at time. (See *Teeth.*)

Emerging from dark recesses to forage, the rat and mouse both have a reputation for occult knowledge and prescience. (The trope of rats fleeing a doomed ship reflects a folk belief in the animal's foresight.) In India the rat is associated with Ganesha, the Hindu god of learning; in Japan the rat is an attribute of Daikokuten, a god of wealth and wisdom. In related symbolism, mice were once used for divination in Africa as "they were believed to understand the mysteries of the underworld" [Tresidder].

Outside of Asia the rat is hated and feared as an icon of filth and pestilence. Although not understood at the time, the Black Death—spread by rats with infected fleas—killed an estimated 50 million people during the 14th century. (Europe alone lost a third of its population between 1347 and 1351.) The fear of large rat populations in dense, urban environments continues to resonate in the Occident: in 2015 the city of New York devoted $2.9 million of its annual budget to rat abatement. By contrast, some temples in India offer sanctuary and food to rats as part of Hindu religious observances.

1

1

In this protest poster published by the Women's Social and Political Union, a ruthless cat grips its prey: a limp woman seeking the right to vote. The policy of releasing jailed suffragettes weakened by hunger strikes—only to rearrest them once recovered—became known as "The Cat and Mouse Act." England, 1914.

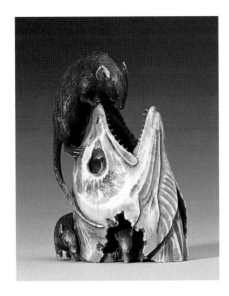

2

A *netsuke* comprised of three rats feasting on the remains of a fish head. One rat peers into the open mouth of the fish, creating an image of dualism: dark and light, heat and cold, life and death. Although associated with disease and mortality, the rat's ability to survive makes it a symbol of tenacity. Japan, 18th–19th century.

3

The infamous Rat Fink, created by American hot rodder Ed "Big Daddy" Roth c. 1963. Embodying the iconoclasm of Southern California's Kustom Kar culture, Rat Fink is the metaphorical evil twin of that other Southern California rodent, Mickey Mouse. Contemporary tin sign.

4

The stuff of children's nightmares: the Mouse King, from a 2011 staging of "The Nutcracker." The Mouse King's seven heads and seven crowns link him to the apocalyptic Beast described in the biblical Book of Revelation. A performance by the English National Ballet, recorded by British photographer Patrick Baldwin.

5

A well-fed, pampered mouse is offered a fan and plucked goose by her servant, a cat, in this ink drawing from Thebes, Egypt. In what may be a satire of the Egyptian ruling class, the noble mouse represents the hope that even the impossible may yet prove possible. Limestone ostracon, c. 1295–1075 BCE.

BAT

Little understood and even feared in medieval Europe, the bat was regarded as a kind of "failed" bird, one of Nature's misbegotten creatures. (In Germany it is known as *fledermaus,* or winged mouse.) Its featherless wings were seen as unnatural and thus malefic, and the batwing is a common attribute of devils and demons in medieval art. (Heavenly angels, by contrast, are given white, feathered wings.)

Ancient Mayans associated the nocturnal, cave-dwelling bat with darkness and the underworld, and so with death. The Cama-Zotz, or Death Bat, is a Mayan god of the underworld linked with decapitation and human sacrifice. The Zotzil tribe in particular considered the bat a god, and their reverence for it is reflected in their name: the Zotzil are the Bat People; their city is Tzinacantlan, or Bat City.

The vampire bat of Central and South America is emblematic of a parasitic lust for life: its survival depends on its lapping up the lifeblood of its hosts. Its feeding habits—preying on unsuspecting victims at night, while they sleep—have erotic implications that are echoed in Bram Stoker's 1897 horror novel *Dracula.*

In Chinese, the sound *fu* can be understood as both "bat" and "blessing." The bat is thus a symbol of good luck in China, and it is used in combination with other homophones to convey coded messages of good wishes. For instance, a bat (*fu*) shown upside down (*dao*) sounds like the phrase *fu dao,* or "blessings have arrived."

1

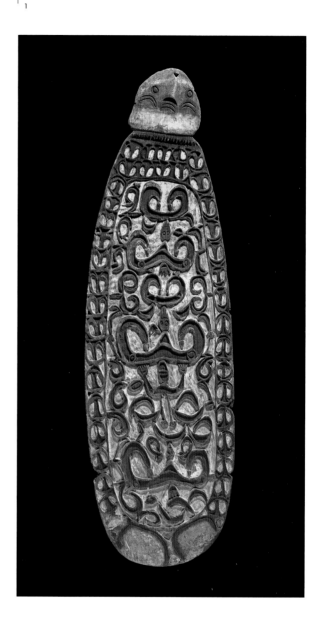

1
This carved wooden shield features a central motif of flying foxes—the world's largest bat. To the warriors of Melanesia, fruit-eating bats symbolized the practice of headhunting; as the fruit is to the tree, so is the head to the body. West Papua, New Guinea, 1960s.

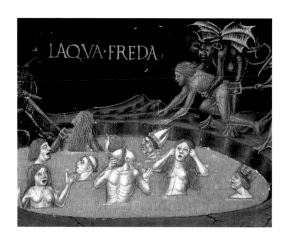

2
A Mimbres bird-headed bat with crosses may reflect the influence of Mayan funerary iconography in which infernal "killer bats" are depicted with crossed bones on their wings. Black-on-white painted bowl, c. 750–1100 CE.

3
This ceramic flute may have been used by Central American shamans to entreat bat spirits in order to harness the bat's seeming powers of night vision. To play the flute one must first invert it, thereby mimicking the bat's natural roosting behavior. Costa Rica, Greater Nicoya culture, 300 BCE–500 CE.

4
The depiction of five bats (*wufu*) is an auspicious motif in Chinese culture as it is homophonous with the phrase "five blessings." The Five Blessings are wishes for a long life, wealth, health, a love of virtue, and a peaceful death. A contemporary ceramic roof tile from the Lan Su Chinese Garden, Portland, Oregon.

5
Web-footed, bat-winged demons mete out the punishment of cold water to sinners in this 15th-century ecclesiastic manuscript illumination by Italian painter Cristoforo De Predis. In Christian iconography a bat's wings signify evil. DETAIL

EGG

Like the seed within its fruit or a child in utero, the avian egg suggests potential; a promise of future life, temporarily held in suspension. The Egyptian glyph for the sun, a dot within a circle, "may have typified the seed within the egg, the 'orphic egg,' symbol of the universe" [Hornung]. The overlapping narratives of egg, seed, womb, and sun reinforce the egg's symbolism as a point of origin or genesis. (See *Fruit; Sun; Concentric Circles*.)

The idea that the world originated from an egg is expressed in the creation myths of Egypt, Phoenicia, Greece, India, China, Japan, Peru, and Polynesia. The physical form of the egg can be seen as the cosmos in miniature: when the shell is divided, the upper half forms the dome of the heavens and the lower half the earth; the golden yolk, suspended between them, shines like a sun. To crack open an egg is to symbolically reenact the moment of the world's birth.

The egg is an Occidental, pre-Christian symbol of fertility, new life, and rebirth. The moon goddess Oestra and her egg-laying hare—now known as the Easter bunny—were central to Germanic spring equinox celebrations. After the advent of Christianity, however, the egg became equated not with the earth's spring regeneration but with the resurrection of Christ. (See *Hare*.)

In Chinese tradition the *yin* earth and *yang* heavens are hatched from a primordial egg. The egg thus becomes a symbol of totality, an exemplar of oppositional yet balanced forces. This sense of totality or wholeness is bolstered by a paradox: although the egg is a symbol of female fertility, its ovoid form approximates the sperm-producing male testis.

1

1

The Virgin in the Egg depicts Mary, the mother of the Christ, contained within an ethereal, cloud-like egg. The egg acts to preserve Mary's purity by physically isolating her from all contact—the one exception being a divine fingertip. The white egg, a symbol of perfection, may also allude to the Roman Catholic doctrine of Mary's Immaculate (i.e. without stain) Conception. Spain, c. 1650, oil on wood.

2

Associated with the birdman cult at Orongo, this ovoid boulder may depict the Oceanic creator god Makemake, who holds the origin of the cosmos—an egg—in his outstretched palm. Easter Island (Rapa Nui), Polynesia, c. late 18th to mid-19th century.

3

A poster announcing a 1972 showing of the film *Der Blaue Engel* by American designer David Lance Goines. The egg, ominously placed on an anvil, serves as a metaphor for the heart and the potential dangers of an asymmetric love.

4

One hundred and fifty, the hen sings, a portrait of fecundity and abundance by Italian photographer Giulio Parisio, c. 1930. The custom of rolling Easter eggs may originate in the belief that it would transfer the eggs' fertile energies to the land and thus increase agricultural yields.

5

An anthropomorphic egg is equated with vitality and life-force (*"Lebenskraft!"*) in this 1938 poster for Schärdinger-Eier by Austrian artist Lois Gagg. Humpty Dumpty, now fortified by fresh eggs, no longer sits idly on a wall but single-handedly hoists a barbell. DETAIL

BIRD

Aloft and seemingly weightless, the bird in flight defies gravity and moves at will. It represents freedom, certainly, but also liberation from the terrestrial plane and so from the material. The bird thus becomes a symbol of purity, higher consciousness, and ascension. "Intelligence is the swiftest of winged creatures," notes the *Rig Veda*.

Like the butterfly, the bird can embody the immaterial essence of the deceased or signify the presence of deity. The ancient Egyptians depicted the *ba*—"soul" or "spirit"—as a human-headed bird rising from a mummy. The Celtic crow's footprint may represent "the descent of souls into the material world" [Chevalier and Gheerbrant]; similarly, the stylized avian feet on Tuareg shields are apotropaic and may indicate the presence of the vulture war god Izez. (See *Butterfly; Crow/ Raven.*)

The bird moves between the terrestrial and celestial realms, and so was commonly thought of as a divine messenger. Known as "taking the auspices," Roman augurs studied the flight patterns of birds to predict the future. A favorable omen was auspicious, from the Latin *auspex,* meaning "one who observes birds." Feathered cloaks or head-dresses were worn by Celts, Native Americans, and Polynesians, among others, to access the sacred knowledge of birds.

The caged bird can symbolize the mind within its physical body (Plato), or a "kept" man or woman, living well materially but nonetheless lacking in freedom. Maya Angelou's 1969 autobiography *I Know Why the Caged Bird Sings* uses the captive bird as a metaphor for black Americans circumscribed by racism.

1

2

1
This Senufo bird effigy likely represents a hornbill, a symbol of intellectual power to members of the men's secret society, *Poro*. With its phallic beak and rounded belly, the self-impregnating bird is an emblem of procreation and thus of life. Ivory Coast, wood, 20th century.

2
Shortly after Lech Walesa was elected president of the Solidarity labor movement in 1981, the communist-backed Polish government imposed martial law. This anonymous poster was printed in secret in 1982, and mocks "Soviet Peace" as an oxymoronic armored dove.

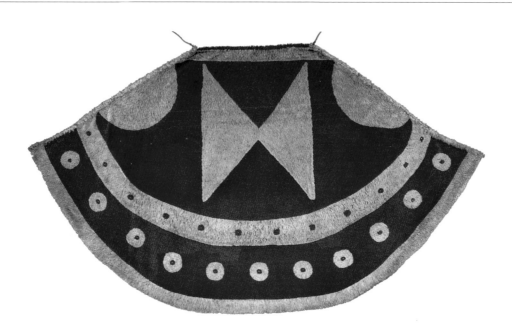

3
In Polynesia the bird was considered a "spiritual messenger"
[MacGregor], a winged mediator
between men and gods. When
entreating the divine, Hawaiian
chiefs would harness the power
of thousands of birds by donning
ceremonial cloaks adorned with
their prized feathers. Hawaii,
before 1780.

4
Once thought to feed its young
with its own blood, the pelican
is a medieval symbol of self-
sacrifice. In this trademark for
Pelikan, maker of inks and pens,
the pelican's blood becomes
synonymous with writing ink. (Its
bill even suggests a pen nib.) Created by German designer O.H.W.
Hadank, 1938.

5
Known to steal shiny objects and
then safeguard them in its nest,
a magpie with a ring is featured
on this 20 pfennig *notgeld* (emergency money) issued by the
German city of Merseburg in 1921.
Perched on a bishop's crosier,
the magpie symbolizes thrift for
a nation on the cusp of historic
hyperinflation.

EAGLE

The eagle is the symbolic equivalent of the lion as both are "kings" of their respective domains. Solar, *yang,* and the attribute and personification of male sky and thunder gods, the eagle is *the* animate icon of celestial power. Reputed to gaze directly at the sun without harm, the eagle's piercing vision also makes it a symbol of extraordinary perception and judgment. (See *Lion; Sun; Eye.*)

To the Plains Indians of North America, the eagle's feathers represented the sun's rays. Wearing an eagle-feather headdress, therefore, was akin to wearing a crown of solar light. (See *Nimbus.*)

The double-headed eagle is a symbolic twin; the repetition multiplies the eagle's potency as an emblem of supreme power. The double-headed eagle can symbolize the Seljuk Empire, Imperial Austria, and Imperial Russia, among others. As the insignia for both the Byzantine and Holy Roman Empires, the two addorsed heads—one facing east, the other west—represented imperial sovereignty over much of the world. The Januslike aspect also implies omniscience. (See *Twins.*)

The eagle in conflict with the serpent is an Aztec symbol linked to the founding of Tenochtitlán in 1325 CE, now known as Mexico City. The two creatures—one celestial, the other chthonic—collectively represent the struggle between heaven and earth, or spirit and matter. The bald eagle, symbol of America, follows the Roman model in which the eagle (i.e. the sky god Jupiter) represents the empire and signals its divine origin. (See *Serpent.*)

OPPOSITE
The Great Seal (after El Lissitsky), a screen-printed montage of imperial symbols by Mark Fox (1998). The decapitated double-headed eagle—a repudiation of czarist rule—is from El Lissitsky's 1923 design of Mayakovsky's book of poetry *Dlia golosa* (*For the Voice*). The other eagle is from the American one-dollar bill.

2
A Tlingit mask, believed to depict an eagle—although the well-defined lines of an owl's beak and supercilium can be seen reversed out of the blue forehead. Tlingit culture is divided into two tribal moieties, the Raven and the Eagle; the mask may relate to the latter. Northwest Coast of America, wood, c. 1820–50.

3
The solar symbolism of the eagle is clearly expressed on these coins from Kyme, Aeolis. The swastika on the coins' reverse—sometimes referred to by numismatists as a "quadrapartite incuse square"—is a rotating symbol suggestive of the diurnal path of the sun. Greek hemiobol, c. 480–450 BCE.

4
Eaglets under the sheltering wings of their mother symbolize the vigilance and fierce protection offered by insurance company Allianz in this 1923 trademark by German designer Karl Schulpig. (The current Allianz trademark still features an eagle, but the eaglets have been excised.)

5
A proposed signet for the American Type Founders Co. by American designer Clarence P. Hornung. The eagle represents America but atypically looks to its left; the ATFC monogram serves as a modern version of a heraldic device on a shield. Published in Hornung's book *Trade-Marks*, 1930.

6
The Aztecs believed that the role of the eagle was to bring the sun god Tonatiuh his daily offering of human hearts. (Without hearts, the sun would fail to rise and the world would end.) This basalt eagle vessel (c. 1500) was used for the cremation of sacrificial hearts. Found near the Templo Mayor, Mexico City.

7
"Bavarians, wake up!," a 1918
election poster for the German
National People's Party. Originally
a Near East symbol of martial
victory, the eagle served as an
imperial emblem of Rome and,
millennia later, Germany. The
eagle's solar nimbus links the
German nation with the divine.
DETAIL

OWL

The nocturnal owl is the symbolic opposite of the diurnal eagle: whereas the eagle is solar and an attribute of male sky gods, the owl is lunar and a familiar of female deities or of male gods of the underworld. Certain species of owl nest in underground burrows, which no doubt contribute to the bird's chthonic associations. (See *Eagle*.)

In Egyptian, Aztec, Hindu, Chinese, Japanese, and Celtic traditions the owl is a bird of the dead whose cries presage evil tidings or imminent death. The Chinese hear in the owl's hooting the exhortation to "Dig, dig," and so interpret the bird's call to mean that a grave will soon be required. The Welsh name for owl is *aderyn y corff,* or corpse bird.

The owl's huge eyes allow it to see and hunt in near total darkness, an ability that suggests supernatural vision and a wisdom that "penetrates the darkness of ignorance" [Matthews]. The raptor's senses are sharpened by its distinctive facial disk, which functions like a parabolic antenna, collecting and focusing light and sound waves for its eyes and ears. Perhaps because of its night vision, the Plains Indians of North America saw the owl as a spirit guide for the recently deceased.

It is largely because of the owl's association with Athena, the Greek goddess of wisdom and learning, that the bird was viewed favorably in Greece and Rome, and later, in Europe. The identification of Athena with the owl is so complete that the goddess was referred to as Athena *Glaukopis,* or Athena Owl-eyed.

1

1
As an avatar of erudition, the owl is frequently used to represent schools, publishers, and libraries. Perched above the door, this 1938 metal raptor guards the entrance to the fifth-floor reading room at the United States Library of Congress. Its spiraling eyes suggest (intellectual) growth, as does the emanating solar disk framing its head. The sun's rays *illuminate.* Pierson & Wilson, architects; photograph by Carol M. Highsmith, 2007.

2

A horizontal slit-drum features a low-relief carving of a horned owl with enlarged, skeletal eye sockets and an open beak. In Aztec culture the owl is a bird of ill omen associated with Mictlantecuhtli, the owl-feathered god of the dead. In this context the sound of the drum may be analogous to the call of the owl and, by extension, the vision (or revelation) of the death god. Mexico, carved wood, c. 1300–1521 CE.

3

On this bookplate by Ukrainian artist Viktor Usolkin, an owl attends a pipe-smoking Satan in his personal library. There is a price to be paid for the owl's occult wisdom: the notice below the bird can be understood as "Books only sold in exchange for souls." Linocut, c. 1960–70.

4

This terracotta drinking cup features two symbols associated with Athens: the owl and the olive. The owl was sacred to Athena; the olive tree was her gift to the city. The owl-and-olive motif also appears on the Athenian tetradrachm, and the silver coin is still known as a *glaux*, or owl. Greek, 450 BCE.

CROW/RAVEN

Iconically black, raucous, and at times brazen, the crow and raven are polyvalent symbols: associated with wisdom, but also considered birds of ill omen. As oracular birds they serve as messengers for gods in Mayan, Japanese, and Norse mythology. The Norse deity Odin relies on a pair of talking ravens—*Hugin* (Mind) and *Munin* (Memory)—to feed him news; ravens are likewise sacred to Apollo, the Greek god of prophecy.

The birds' omnivorous eating habits, which apparently include carrion and battlefield corpses, cast the crow and raven as odious representatives of misfortune, war, and death. The raven is an attribute of the Greek goddess of war Athena; the name of the Celtic war-goddess *Badb* means Carrion Crow, and the goddess may take the form of a raven during battle.

In medieval Europe, Christians believed the raven to be a malefic entity, a proxy for the devil himself; its reputed habit of plucking out eyes was analogous to Satan "blinding" sinners. The bird was also associated with the sin of gluttony, which may explain the 15th-century term "ravenous," meaning voracious or rapacious. (By 1530 the verb "raven" would be synonymous with despoil and plunder.)

A solitary crow or raven was once considered an ominous sign; greater numbers would only amplify this perception. (A gathering of crows is known as "a murder"; a group of ravens is "an unkindness" or "a conspiracy.") British director Alfred Hitchcock exploits this historical unease in his 1963 film *The Birds* with a scene in which a flock of crows attacks a classroom of terrified children.

1
The crow and heron are a familiar juxtaposition in Japanese art as exemplars of *yin* and *yang* dualism: black and white, night and day, male and female, the crow "mischievous and chattering" and the heron "serious and silent" [Cooper]. Japanese lacquer box, Edo period, 19th century.

2
To the Native Americans of the Pacific Northwest, Raven is a trickster figure not unlike Prometheus in Greek tradition. This carved wooden mask illustrates the creation myth of Raven stealing daylight for the world; he carries the red disk of the sun within his beak. Nuxalk, Central Coast, British Columbia, c. 1860–80.

3

4

5

3
Although highly intelligent—it uses tools and can learn to distinguish between individual human faces—the crow is largely viewed as a despised pest, appropriate for target practice. "Target No. 7" from Sears, Roebuck & Co., offset lithography, c. 1950s. DETAIL

4
A native of Scotland, Dr. James Crow is the namesake of the Kentucky sour mash bourbon known as Old Crow. (Dr. Crow's whiskey is "old" because it is aged.) Used as a trademark and mnemonic, this anthropomorphic crow sports a top hat and spats to suggest urbane sophistication. Ceramic, c. 1950s.

5
The implied equivalence between African Americans and crows in popular (white) imagination in the 19th century is exemplified by the racist photograph "Me and Jim." ("Jim Crow" was a common racial slur used to describe black Americans after 1838.) American studio photographer E.C. Dana created this image around 1895.

BEE

Like the butterfly, the bee can represent the soul. Its reemergence in the spring following its annual winter dormancy renders the bee a sign of cyclical death and regeneration, and hence immortality. To the Greeks the bee served as a mnemonic for Persephone; to early Christians, for Christ's resurrection. (See *Butterfly*.)

Solar, dusted with golden pollen, the bee was an emblem of life and power in ancient Egypt. (It was said that bees originated from the tears of the sun god Ra.) In emulation of the 5th-century Frankish king Childeric I, Napoléon Bonaparte's 1804 coronation was replete with bee iconography. The new Emperor of France sat on a red velvet cushion embroidered with one monumental, golden bee.

The bee's colony represents order and industry, and is a common allegory of community. Mormons have used the hive to symbolize their church since the 1840s; around the same time the international labor movement published Karl Marx in the newspaper *The Beehive*. More recently the hive has been likened to the internet, although some see this as a pejorative. In his 2010 book *You Are Not A Gadget,* Jaron Lanier writes about the internet's "hive mind" and the cultural implications of privileging aggregated, collective "wisdom" over individual creative expression.

Erroneously thought to reproduce asexually, the bee came to symbolize chastity in the Middle Ages. (Depictions of the Virgin Mary sometimes include bees for this reason.) The bee's transformation of nectar into honey was considered equally mysterious: untouched by human hands in its making, honey was seen as "pure" and as a food befitting gods.

1

1
The Honeycomb Vase "Made by Bees" by Dutch industrial designer Tomáš Libertíny of Studio Libertíny (2006), fabricated by 40,000 bees over the course of a week. Libertíny refers to his apiarian collaboration as "slow prototyping." In the context of the vase's manufacture, the bee and its wax are signifiers of nature that yield unpredictable, imperfect, and ultimately singular results.

3

4

2

The Honeycomb Apartments, a "social housing" project designed by OFIS arhitekti. Intended to house young families and couples in an affordable way, this apartment complex uses the modular construction of the beehive to maximize space and create community. Izola, Slovenia, 2003–05.

3

German architect and designer Peter Behrens' 1907 trademark for Allgemeine Elektricitäts-Gesellschaft. Behrens uses the hexagonal honeycomb cell as a metaphor for AEG's disparate but related enterprises, which ranged from the manufacture of industrial steam turbines to electric household appliances.

4

The golden bee signifies sweetness on this blind-embossed poster stamp for a 1925 sugar exhibition in Magdeburg, Germany. The bee was originally designed by Wilhelm Deffke of the studio Wilhelmwerk in 1922. Note the letter M (for Magdeburg) formed by the bee's legs.

BUTTERFLY

The Greek word *psyche* can be translated as soul, breath, or butterfly. The ephemeral nature of the insect, as insubstantial as breath, make it an apt symbol of fleeting human life. The Aztecs saw in the butterfly the exhaled soul of a dead warrior, or of a mother who died in childbirth.

The metamorphosis of the butterfly—from earth-bound grub to winged sprite—is analogous to a number of life's transformations, including the shift from childhood to adulthood, or from ignorance to wisdom. Metamorphosis can also represent the liberation of the soul from the body at death and its migration from the terrestrial plane to the celestial. It is this latter view that informs Christian iconography in which the butterfly is a symbol of resurrection, rebirth, and thus immortality.

Whereas the moth is generally nocturnal, the diurnal butterfly navigates by sunlight. Its flight, marked by flashes of iridescent color, conjures the flickering of firelight. It is for this reason, perhaps, that the butterfly embodied fire to the Celts and solar fire to the Aztecs.

In Japan the butterfly symbolizes female vanity and young women in general; its restless fluttering is likened to a geisha or to a fickle lover. Conversely, in China and Korea the butterfly is seen as a young man who flits from female flower to flower, looking for love. Two butterflies represent conjugal bliss throughout the Orient.

1

1
A basalt warrior erected atop Pyramid B at Tula, the Toltec capital of pre-Columbian Mexico, c. 900 CE. The butterfly pectoral that shields the warrior's heart is a manifestation of the Meso-american deity Quetzalcoatl. In this context the butterfly is apotropaic and indicates the god's protection.

2
Virtue of Blue, a chandelier comprised of 502 butterfly-shaped solar silicon cell panels by Jeroen Verhoeven of the Dutch design collective Demakersvan (2010). While the solar panels could no doubt assume an abstract shape for the chandelier to function, the mass of butterflies immediately creates a connection between

solar power (i.e. sustainable energy) and the world's ecosystems. To the Bwa people of Burkina Faso, the swarms of butterflies that accompany the return of the spring rainy season signify new life; one can see related symbolism at work in *Virtue of Blue's* fabricated butterflies.

3
A butterfly design from Sikyatki earthenware, created sometime before 1500 CE. Based on a series of interlocking triangles, the design is structurally related to a Hopi glyph for "woman." As the butterfly signified fertility and life to the Hopi, there may be a conceptual link between the two.

4
A golden butterfly is encircled by a golden ouroboros on the tomb of German composer Ludwig van Beethoven (1770–1827). Both are symbols of continuous regeneration and immortality, and imply that the composer's music is timeless. Zentralfriedhof cemetary, Vienna, Austria. DETAIL

5
American dancer Loie Fuller in a photograph by fellow American Frederick W. Glasier, c. 1902. Fuller gained fame in the 1890s at Paris' Folies-Bergère for her dramatic dances with billowing silk, among them "The Butterfly."

Spinning silk and then weaving it into a web, the spider is an attribute of female divinities who weave the strands of mankind's destiny, among them Neith (Egyptian), Ishtar (Babylonian), and Athena and the Fates (Greek). (The word "weave" is from the Greek *hyphos,* or web.) In some traditions the spider is the creator of the cosmos, using the stuff of its own body to construct the fabric of reality. Conversely, in India the spider weaves a world not of reality but of illusion, or *maya.* The insubstantiality of the spider's web is analogous to the unreliability of the world of appearances.

The spider within its web is both a life and death symbol. While the web radiates from the spider at its center like the life-giving sun, it ultimately serves as a labyrinth or trap with death at its core. The spider's single thread of silk can also be seen as an umbilicus, the life-giving link to a mother or creator; and yet this thread also binds prey to predator. (See *Sun.*)

As the female spider is known to periodically cannibalize her smaller male counterpart after mating, the spider can symbolize treachery and, in particular, feminine wiles. In Japan, the *joro* spider—literally, courtesan spider—is named after *Jorogumo,* a shape-shifting woman who traps and seduces men, only to feast on them when she reveals herself to be an arachnid. (See *Fox.*)

In the folktales of West Africa, the spider Anansi is a male trickster figure who outwits larger foes through his wisdom and cunning.

1

1
German designer Willi Petzold harnesses the mythological link between the spider and weaving in this poster for a 1924 Textile Exhibition. With a spool of thread as its body, Petzold's spider appears to be weaving itself into existence, like some primeval god of creation.

2
The headdress of this Bamum helmet mask features a stylized spider formed of glass beads and cowrie shells. To the Bamum of Cameroon, the spider is a symbol of wisdom and is believed to mediate between humans and their creator. This mask was made prior to 1880.

3
Comprising two numeral sevens, the US Army's 7th Infantry Division has used an hourglass insignia since 1918. In time the hourglass became associated with the mark on the venomous black widow spider, and now symbolizes lethal force. (The division's motto is "Light, Silent, and Deadly.")

4
The Diné (or Navajo) people of the American Southwest maintain that the legendary Spider Woman taught them the art of weaving. The Spider Woman Cross on this blanket may represent the crux of the weaver's creative act: the crossing of horizontal and vertical threads. Navajo, Germantown wool.

5
More than thirty feet high, artist Louise Bourgeois' *Maman* is a monumental "ode" to the artist's mother Josephine, who worked as a weaver. With its central sac of eggs the giant spider conjures both fecundity and instinctive maternal protection. *Maman* outside the Kunsthalle in Hamburg, Germany, 2012.

FISH

A syllogism: if fish are symbolic proxies for water, and if water is life, then *fish are life*. Highly prolific, with some species capable of producing a million or more eggs at a time, fish embody female fertility and reflect the procreative, life-sustaining, and regenerative powers of water. (See *Water*.)

In Middle Eastern and Asian iconography a pair of fish can signify felicity, marital union, and fecundity. (The two-fish motif appears on 19th-century illuminated Jewish marriage contracts or *ketubah*.) In Buddhism, twin fish symbolize freedom from restraint; in Hinduism, "two fishes touching nose-to-tail depict the yoni" [Cooper]. Three fish forming an equilateral triangle can serve as a mnemonic for the Christian concept of the Trinity. (See *Triangle*.)

The sexual symbolism of the fish is both male and female. While its form approximates the phallus, the fish is more often associated with lunar and mother goddesses, and served as an emblem of ocean-born Venus. (In ancient Rome, fish were ritually eaten in honor of the goddess of love and fertility on *dies Veneris,* or Friday.) When drawn with two linear, overlapping arcs, the fish's body creates an almond silhouette known as a *mandorla* that suggests the vulva; using straight lines produces a lozenge that is symbolically equivalent. (See *Lozenge*.)

The Chinese word for "fish," *yu,* is a homophone with the word "surplus." As a symbol of abundance and happiness, fish are eaten at Chinese New Year feasts in the hope that doing so will ensure a prosperous future.

1

1
Admired for the vigor of its upstream migrations, the Asian carp is a symbol of fortitude—a male virtue in Japan. Carp standards are flown for the Boy's Festival in this woodblock print by *ukiyo-e* artist Ando Hiroshige. *Suido Bridge and Surugadai, No. 48 from One Hundred Famous Views of Edo,* 1857.

2
Three perch swim in the circle of life on this Greek fish-plate from Apulia, Italy. A solar rosette is ringed by a repeating wave pattern; three limpets join with the central motif to form an implied triskele, a three-legged Aegean symbol of life and cyclical regeneration. Red-figure pottery, c. 4th century BCE.

3
Synodontis is a genus of catfish that swims upside-down at the surface of the water to feed. Appearing dead yet clearly alive, the fish may have suggested life after death to ancient Egyptians. Young women wore amulets of the fish as a precaution against drowning. Amethyst and gold, c. 1980–1760 BCE.

4
An ambulatory fish confidently strides ashore in this trademark for surfwear company Gotcha Sportswear. The symbol is a playful inversion of the mermaid and merman archetypes in which a human's upper body is paired with a fishtail. Created by American designer Jay Vigon, 1985.

5
The zodiacal sign of the constellation Pisces from an illuminated French psalter, c. 1250–60. Two stellar fish, swimming in opposite directions, signify the concepts of departure and return, and of past and future. Tempera colors, gold leaf, and ink on parchment.
DETAIL

OCTOPUS

Three-fifths of the octopus' neurons are in its extremities, not its brain, allowing the eight tentacles a striking degree of independent "thought" and agency. The helical form of these tentacles as they coil and uncoil link the octopus with the life symbolism of the spiral and vortex, and "represents the unfolding of creation from the mystic center" [Fontana]. (See *Spiral*.)

Multi-limbed, cold-blooded, and utterly alien, a monstrous octopus is often used as a symbol of menace to induce fear—especially when that menace is comprised of disparate but interconnected entities. By the late 19th century the octopus emerged in the Occident as a potent evocation of the long reach of industrial monopolies and predatory capitalism. Before its forced dissolution in 1911, the Standard Oil trust exemplified the monopoly-as-octopus analogy.

In tandem with its use as a cautionary symbol of corporate capitalism, the octopus is used in propaganda and on maps, in particular, to identify avaricious, land-grabbing countries. Britain, Prussia, Russia, Germany, Japan, America, and China have all been depicted as octopods with imperialist tendencies.

The amorous octopus, groping a beautiful young female diver, is a familiar motif in Japanese erotic art where it finds expression in 18th- and 19th-century carved *netsuke* and *shunga* prints, perhaps most memorably in Katsushika Hokusai's woodblock print of 1814. It is worth noting that *tako,* the Japanese word for *octopus,* can be playfully understood as a homonym with *takou,* meaning great happiness. In Hokusai's print the octopus may do more than simply serve as a proxy for the phallus—it may embody the happy prospect of female orgasm.

1

JAPAN MENACES WORLD TRADE

1
"Japan Menaces World Trade," a pamphlet issued by the British Ministry of Information in 1944 in response to Japanese control of the Far East. The octopus—symbolizing Japanese imperialism—is superimposed on a rising sun like a long-limbed spider on its web, monopolizing raw materials as if they were prey.

3

4

2
In Germany the term *daten-krake* or data octopus is used to describe corporations that harvest the private data of their users. "Freedom not Fear," a 2009 protest against surveillance that was staged in Berlin, featured an effigy of a *datenkrake* created by German artist Peter Ehrentraut.

3
Inky, the mascot and trademark of CustomInk, a producer of made-to-order, screen-printed T-shirts. While octopus ink isn't used as a dye, another cephalo-pod, the cuttlefish, was called *sepia* by the Romans who used its brown ink for writing. Inky was created by Charles S. Anderson Design in 2010.

4
An octopus with eight exuber-antly undulating arms covers the surface of this Greek krater. Tentacles spill out of the cepha-lopod like water gushing from a spring—which may be the point. As these vessels were used for the mixing and serving of wine at symposia, the design may be making an implicit comparison between the body of the animal and the body of the krater. And, like an octopus' treacher-ous limbs, rivulets of wine may threaten to ensnare the drinking party's guests. Rhodes, painted pottery, c. 1375–1300 BCE.

SEASHELL

The seashell is the exoskeleton of a mollusk, the durable husk of a marine snail. Originating in the ocean, the shell shares water's associations with creation and procreation, genetrix and matrix. Combined with physical characteristics that can suggest female genitalia, the shell is an emblem of fecundity and life, and by extension, felicity and prosperity. (See *Water.*)

The cowrie shell, in particular, is an erotically charged symbol. Prized as an apotropaic ornament in Egypt, Oceania, and Africa, it was used throughout the Indian Ocean as a form of currency. By the late 17th century, European traders had so flooded the African continent with imported cowries that they succeeded in wresting control of tribal economies. Among other goods the cowrie was traded for slaves, thereby rendering the shell a historical marker of colonial exploitation.

In Hindu tradition the conch shell, or *shankha* in Sanskrit, is associated with the sacred sound *Om:* the primordial vibration of creation that emerges from Vishnu's conch when it is sounded. In Islamic thought the convolutions of the conch suggest the ear, or hearing; the pearl within the conch is the spoken (divine) word. The conch shell thus "symbolizes concentration upon the Word" [Chevalier and Gheerbrant].

As the shell is all that remains of its former inhabitant, like the skull it can serve as a momento mori. In this regard the shell—symbol of life—also signifies death. In Christendom the empty shell is a symbol of the resurrection, analogous to the empty tomb.

1

2

1
William Golding's 1954 novel *Lord of the Flies* chronicles the struggle of marooned schoolboys to create a society in the absence of adults. The character Ralph cradles a conch—symbol of authority and civility—in British director Harry Hook's 1990 film adaptation.

2
This wooden baby carrier is blanketed with protective carvings, including three menacing figures, their enormous, unblinking eyes inlaid with disks of shell. In some traditions shells are believed to ward off the evil eye, and so their use as a material is likely apotropaic. Kayanic people, Borneo, Indonesia, date unknown.

3

Swiss architect Le Corbusier was profoundly influenced by naturally occurring proportional relationships, in particular by the growth pattern of the spiraling nautilus shell. Le Corbusier used the nautilus as inspiration for his proposed Museum of Unlimited Growth (1931), and depicted it in other projects as an icon of the golden ratio. Untitled lithograph from Le Corbusier's *Poem of the Right Angle*, 1955.

4

The goddess of love emerges from a seashell in *The Birth of Venus*, a painting by French artist Odilon Redon, c. 1912. The shell's elliptical silhouette and luminous interior create a nimbus similar to the *mandorla* surrounding Byzantine depictions of the Christ. This shell is maternal matrix, life, light, and utterly sacred.

5

A steel 20-cedis coin from Ghana, Africa, 1995. Cowrie shells were formerly used as money in the Asante region, hence the coin's design and name. (*Cedi* is the Ghanaian word for cowrie.) The cowrie's distinctive opening has been chastely rendered at an oblique angle to neuter its sexual symbolism.

SNAIL

Positioned at the tips of two tentacles, the land snail's eyes telescope in and out of sight like the waxing and waning moon. The snail is thus associated with the lunar phases, and is itself a symbol of cyclical renewal and rebirth. That the snail reliably retires to its moon-like shell also contributes to this symbolism. (See *Moon.*)

With its metaphorical house perched upon its back, the snail is a model of self-sufficiency. Jacobus Boschius' 1701 *Symbolographia* includes an engraving of a snail with the legend *Mecum Omnia,* an abbreviation of the Latin maxim that means "All that's mine I carry with me."

Moist and voluptuous in its movements, the snail is a fertility symbol that conjures both female and male genitalia. While its undulating foot and secretions are analogous to the vulva, the snail's head suggests a tumescent phallus. (Its tentacles also give it the appearance of "horns," a sign of male virility.) As many land snails are hermaphroditic, the intermixing of female and male sexual symbolism is apt. (See *Bull; Horns/Antlers.*)

In addition to sharing the land snail's lunar and fertility symbolism, the murex marine snail is linked with royal power. The murex secretes a compound that was used in antiquity to create the color Tyrian purple. The dye was rare and exceedingly expensive, with approximately 12,000 of the mollusks yielding a mere 1.5 grams of dye. The color was reserved for nobility in the Roman and Byzantine Empires, and medieval depictions of venerated figures often use purple cloth to signal rank or importance.

1

1
This Javanese crown top—or *usnisha* cover—is designed to conceal the topknot of a person or statue. The pattern of spirals may reference snails who are said to have crawled onto the Buddha's head to shelter him from the sun. The snail is a model of piety and sacrifice in this context. Indonesia, gold, c. 650–1000 CE.

2

A proposed cover design for the book *L'Éloge de la Lenteur* or *In Praise of Slowness*, by American illustrator Ward Schumaker, 2005. The meandering snail, unhurried but purposeful, is a charming evocation of French author Carl Honoré's paean to slow eating, slow reading, and slow living.

3

REgeneration: fifty monumental snails occupy the roof of the Duomo di Milano in this 2012 installation by the international collective Cracking Art Group. The 14th-century cathedral is in need of repairs and renewal; the snails—made of recycled plastic—illustrate the potential of material rebirth.

4

Schneckenreiter or Snail Rider, by Austrian designer Michael Powolny. A prepubescent male nude rides a snail whose erect head suggests an animate phallus. The boy's youthful transport—the snail—will later be substituted for the transport of sexual ecstasy. Wiener Keramik, c. 1907.

5

The snail's helical shell links it to the spiral and whorl, symbols of dynamism, potentiality, and life. This ancient Mexican clay stamp design depicts a cross-section of a mollusk shell—likely a conch— that reveals a spiral within its interior. Documented by Jorge Enciso in the 1940s.

FROG/TOAD

Largely nocturnal and living in or near water, the frog and toad are underworld symbols of primeval creation, female fertility, and maternity. Considered lunar and *yin,* the amphibians are associated with the renewing properties of spring rains and, in Egypt, with the annual flooding of the Nile. The tadpole is so abundant that ancient Egyptians used a hieroglyph of the nascent frog to indicate the number 100,000.

The frog is the emblem of Heket, the Egyptian goddess of pregnancy and childbirth, and so came to symbolize birth itself. As a metamorphic creature, the frog also signifies bodily transformation. Egyptians wrapped faience frog amulets with mummies as symbols of rebirth, and later Christianized Egyptians understood the frog as a mnemonic for the resurrected Christ.

In medieval Europe the frog and toad were believed to be the familiars of witches, with the toad, in particular, seen as the incarnation of the devil or of an unclean spirit. That some toads are "horned" or emit noxious chemicals would only reinforce the amphibian's malefic reputation. By contrast, pre-Columbian Mayans and Aztecs regarded the toad as a rain god, thereby associating it with life and fertility. The ancient Chinese held similar views, believing the toad capable of coaxing rain from the sky.

In Vietnam, the frog's incessant nocturnal croaking is likened to the repetitive instruction of a dull schoolteacher. To early Christians, a chorus of frogs evoked the preaching of heretical doctrine.

OPPOSITE
This ocarina likely depicts *Bufo marinus,* a giant toad valued by Mesoamericans for the hallucinogen bufotenine that it secretes. The flowing shapes emerging from both sides of the toad's head may refer to the psychoactive toxin. Slip-painted ceramic, Mexico, Southern Veracruz, Nopiloa, 700–900 CE.

2
In global decline since the 1980s and exhibiting a range of developmental abnormalities, frogs and other amphibians have emerged as contemporary symbols of environmental degradation. (Frogs are extremely sensitive to water-borne contaminants.) A trematode cyst-infected Pacific Treefrog with extra limbs, 1998.

3
Crapaud (Acrobatic Frog), from
the series *Carnaval à Jacmel* by
American photographer Phyllis
Galembo (1998). The frog and
crapaud, or toad, both symbolize
metamorphosis, and the Haitian
revelers who masquerade as
amphibians are similarly transfig-
ured—if only temporarily.

4
The toad embodies slimy repulsiveness in this 1936 photomontage by German artist John Heartfield. In "Voice from the Swamp," published in *Arbeiter-Illustrierte-Zeitung* (or *The Workers Pictorial Newspaper*), Heartfield parodies Nazi theories of Aryan racial superiority as the croaking of an inbred toad.

5
The underside of this terra-cotta frog reveals a nude female in the squatting position of childbirth—possibly Prithvi Mata, the Hindu earth goddess. As both the frog and Prithvi are linked with fertility and mud (or moist earth), the use of clay for the figurine is apt. Mathura, India, 2nd century CE.

6
The frog's identification with female generative power is made explicit by this motif in which the amphibian's torso is comprised of nested lozenges. From a Bagam wooden sheath, Cameroon; linocut by American designer Geoffrey Williams, 1971.

7
The frog is a symbol of good luck and safe passage in Japan. As the Japanese word for "frog," *kaeru*, is a homophone with the verb "to return," the Japanese traveler may carry a tiny frog amulet in the belief that doing so will ensure a safe return home. Contemporary painted ceramic.

TORTOISE

The tortoise (or turtle) is an auspicious life symbol throughout Asia. Considered *yin,* the reptile is associated with water, female generative powers, and the creation and fixity of the world. With some specimens living 150 years or more, the tortoise is a symbol of longevity, immortality, and thus wisdom. The enigmatic markings on its shell are likened to maps or writing—further "evidence" of the tortoise's sapience.

Its arched shell evokes a mountain or, in the case of a partially submerged turtle, an island, which may explain the range of myths linking the turtle to a sacred mountain and to the origin of the world. (Native Americans referred to North America as "Turtle Island," for example.) Seemingly indestructible—few natural predators can crush a mature tortoise's shell—the animal was believed to underpin the world, and so can signify stability or imperviousness. (See *Elephant.*)

In Hindu and Chinese lore the tortoise is the cosmos in miniature: its convex carapace is likened to the dome of heaven; its breastplate—or plastron—is analogous to the earthly plane. Sandwiched between, the reptile is seen as a mediator between the celestial and terrestrial; between gods and men. It is for this reason, perhaps, that the ancient Chinese used tortoise plastrons for divination, interpreting hairline cracks on the shell's surface. (The tortoise was said to "speak" when its heated shell cracked.)

The tortoise's slow gait makes it a symbol of patience and perseverance. Aesop's fable "The Hare and the Tortoise" concludes with a moral that lauds the tortoise's natural tempo: "Slow and steady wins the race." (See *Snail.*)

1
Originally interred in a shaft tomb, this funerary ceramic depicts a seated musician striking a turtle shell with an antler or bone. Ancient Mesoamericans may have associated the sound of a drummed turtle shell with the rumble of thunder, and thus with life-giving rain. Mexico, Nayarit, 200 BCE–200 CE.

2
The hexagonal plates on the tortoise's shell are called scutes. Three plaited scutes form a stylized tortoise shell on this Japanese family crest, or *mon*. Reputed to live for thousands of years, the tortoise is an emblem of longevity in Japan; its use as a *mon* would be propitious, auguring long life.

3
The shells of two mud turtles form a limestone palette for the preparation and application of kohl. The Nile's mud connoted fertility and regeneration to predynastic Egyptians, and the mud turtles—fused as if mating—likely reinforce the mud's procreative symbolism. Sculpted greywacke with inlays, c. 3650–3500 BCE.

4
The golden *eobo* (royal seal) of Queen Munjeong of Korea. In Chinese thought the tortoise is equated with the north and exemplifies strength and endurance. In this context the reptile may signify the northern kingdom of Korea, whose Joseon dynasty lasted 500 years. Cast bronze with gilding, 16th century.

5
Like Ao, the primordial sea turtle that carries the world on its back, a stone turtle supports a funerary stela at the 1st-century tomb of Chinese nobleman Xiao Xiu. By virtue of the turtle's role as an Atlas, Xiao Xiu's life (and death) are accorded "global" significance. Photograph by French writer Victor Ségalen, 1917.

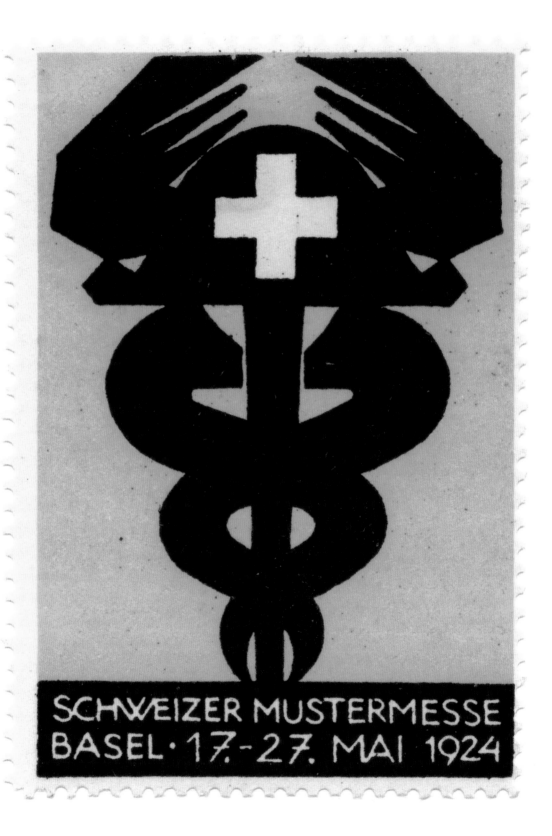

SERPENT

The serpent is "a living line" [Chevalier and Gheerbrant]. Its sinuous form suggests intestines or the umbilicus—the lifeline between a mother and her child—as well as the flow of water or blood. (Mayan iconography depicts "blood serpents" issuing from the necks of decapitated heads.) While it can be emblematic of death due to its venomous bite, the serpent remains first and foremost a primeval life symbol.

Among the Hopi of Arizona and in parts of India, the serpent (*naga* in Sanskrit) is considered a rain-giver. Identification with rain as well as its phallic silhouette make the reptile a symbol of male fertility and sexuality; even the female serpent appears sperm-like when among her nest of eggs.

Because it sheds its skin the serpent symbolizes regeneration and resurrection. In the Sumerian *Epic of Gilgamesh*, for example, a serpent eats a sacred plant that confers immortality and subsequently molts. The ouroboros—a serpent ingesting its own tail—is another manifestation of this idea. Self-impregnating and continually reborn, the ouroboros represents a cycle without end. (See *Circle*.)

The serpent is generally earth-bound—the Latin verb *serpere* means "to creep"—and when paired with the eagle (as on the Mexican flag) the opposing creatures represent the struggle between matter and spirit, or between man's baser and higher instincts. When winged the serpent becomes a dragon, and the chthonic and celestial aspects are fused into one physical form. (See *Eagle.*)

2

OPPOSITE
The caduceus of Mercury, god of commerce, announces the 1924 Swiss Industries Fair on a poster stamp by designer Robert Stöcklin. Two oppositional serpents, separate yet united, create an equilibrium that yields harmony. The two coupling snakes also symbolize fertility.

2
This trademark may be a variation of the Mosaic and Aesculapian staffs of healing, in which a single, living serpent entwines a pole. This serpent is impaled and likely chthonic: "an arrow piercing a serpent is the sun's rays piercing the dark" [Cooper]. German designer J. Ehlers for an unidentified business, c. 1928.

3

The coat of arms of the House of Visconti—14th-century rulers of Milan—is the origin of the mythic serpent on Alfa Romeo's badge. In use by the Italian automaker since 1910, the emblem is an indeterminate symbol; as snakes tend to swallow their prey headfirst, it may depict a symbolic birth rather than a death.

4

As a mark of their faith, members of the Pentecostal Church of God in rural Kentucky handle poisonous snakes in this 1946 photograph by American photojournalist Russell Lee. The life-threatening serpent serves as a concrete test of the believer's faith in his savior.

5

"Join, or Die," American statesman (and printer) Benjamin Franklin's 1754 exhortation to his fellow colonists during the French and Indian War. A rattlesnake with the motto "Don't Tread on Me" will later threaten the British on the Gadsden flag of 1775.

6

The fixed, implacable knight represents stability; ten writhing serpents imply the chaos that will ensue from Germany's loss to its enemies in this WWI poster stamp by Austrian designer Julius Klinger (1914). Klinger will again use a serpent as the symbolic enemy in his "8th War Loan" poster of 1918.

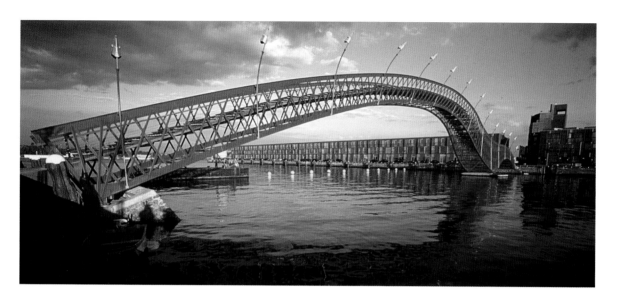

7
Amsterdam's Borneo-Sporen-
burg bridge, popularly known as
the Python Bridge (1998–2001).
This undulating structure
embodies the urban rebirth of
the formerly dilapidated Eastern
Docklands. Conceived by Dutch
urban design and landscape
architectural office, West 8.

8
A diamondback pattern comple-
ments the coiled construction
of this Native American woven
basket, echoing the rattlesnake's
natural form. The diamond—or
lozenge—is an ancient fertility
symbol that references the vulva.
Yokuts, early 20th century.

9
A San Bushman rock painting of
a double-headed horned serpent,
South Africa, documented in a
linocut by American designer
Geoffrey Williams in the 1970s.
Its significance is unclear, but
as there is no tail—or "end"—it
may be a linear expression of the
circular ouroboros.

HAND

EYE

MOUTH/TONGUE

TEETH

FOOT/SHOE

HEART

HAIR

NIMBUS

TWINS

human

HAND

The hand signifies agency, the capacity to engender action. A small or weak hand, such as a child's, signals impotence; an enlarged hand paired with an elongated arm is a sign of power and the greater reach of that power. The English word "left"—from the Old English *lyft*—means weak or useless, and in the Occident the left hand has become synonymous with moral weakness and duplicity. The right hand is the hand of strength, truth, and god.

The open hand is receptive and can symbolize peace or submission. The closed hand is unyielding, defiant, and militant: a red, clenched fist was the symbol of the communist Red Front during their years of conflict with the Nazi Party. The American Black Power movement is identified with the fist as well, perhaps most notably by the gloved fists of Olympic medalists Tommie Smith and John Carlos at the 1968 Mexico City Games. (Their gesture prompted fellow Olympian Jesse Owens to observe: "The only time the black fist has significance is when there's money inside.")

In addition to gestures, the hand communicates via its jewelry or other embellishments: rings can signal marital or economic status, or can indicate membership in a fraternal organization. Among Russian criminals, finger-ring tattoos and other symbols applied to the hands comprise a thief's entire history, and can be read by other thieves as a "passport, case file, awards record, diploma, and epitaph" [Plutser-Sarno]. In this context, the hand functions as an ongoing visual biography.

1

2

1
The Giant Buddha at the Chin Swee Caves Temple in Genting Highlands, Malaysia, displays what is known as the *Vitarka Mudra,* the hand gesture of teaching or discussion. The monumentality and materiality of this *mudra* enrich its meaning: the teachings of Buddha are substantive and enduring.

2
A symbol for the National Campaign Against Youth Violence. The silhouette of an open hand, a universal gesture of nonviolence, is completed by the open wings of a dove—a bird that embodies peace. Peace is not only possible, it is within our grasp. By American designer Felix Sockwell and illustrator Erik Johnson, 1999.

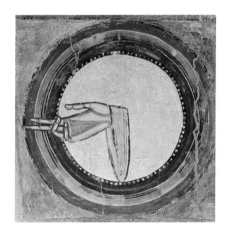

3

Qing Dynasty Empress Cixi's decorative fingernail guards prevent her from performing basic gripping actions, thus ensuring that hands other than her own will be required to perform even the simplest tasks. Cixi's adorned hands are symbols of privilege. China, c. 1903–04.

4

"This is the way to peace—the enemy wants it so!" German designer Lucian Bernhard depicts his countrymen as reluctant combatants in this WWI propaganda poster. The clenched fist is resolute; the gauntlet reinforces the gesture's aggressiveness.
DETAIL

5

The disembodied hand is inherently mythic, and it typically signifies the presence of the supernatural. In *The Hand of God* fresco from Sant Climent deTaüll in Catalonia (c. 1123), a divine fingertip extends beyond its nimbus into secular space and time—but just barely.

6

The solidarity of the Dutch trade union movement is celebrated on this 1989 postage stamp by Dutch designers Lies Ros and Rob Schroeder of Wild Plakken. Hands symbolize work (and workers); freedom of expression is suggested by the open mouths. These hands have voices.

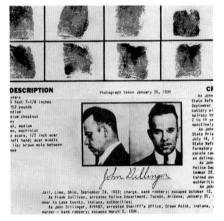

7

This flame-impervious hand is divine, but the model isn't Christian; not only is the hand black, it is a left hand. (The right hand signifies righteousness in Christian art.) Rather, it is likely the hand of the blacksmith Vulcan, Roman god of fire, that proffers "Celestial" razor blades.

8

This Japanese ashtray is an icon of female subservience: the cupped left hand—considered weak and *yin*—waits passively for cigarette ashes or discarded butts. That this is a woman's hand is made clear by the red fingernails; that it is the size of a child's hand only emphasizes its powerlessness.

9

Handprints and fingerprints are markers of authenticity and identity. In an effort to forestall his identification and imprisonment, American bank robber John Dillinger used acid to chemically remove his fingerprints several months after this circular was issued in March 1934. DETAIL

EYE

The eye is a universal symbol of perception, discernment, and intelligence. (Two birds of prey with vision far superior to our own, the solar eagle and lunar owl, are both symbols of wisdom.) The concept of the "third eye" in Buddhism, Hinduism, and other religious practices is predicated on the belief that an inner vision can lead to transcendent wisdom. (See *Eagle; Owl*.)

A disembodied, hovering eye is a symbol of omniscience. It can represent the sun, the all-seeing gaze of the sun god or, in the case of J.R.R. Tolkien's *Lord of the Rings* trilogy, the "Red Eye" of Sauron. In both Christian and Freemason iconography an eye within a triangle is known as the Eye of Providence, an example of which appears within the Great Seal of the United States (1782) on the reverse of the American one-dollar bill. The relationship between eye, sun, and god is evident in the glyph common to all three concepts: a dot enclosed by a circle. (See *Sun; Concentric Circles*.)

A lidless eye cannot close or sleep and is therefore a sign of ceaseless vigilance. Although William Golden's 1951 trademark for Columbia Broadcasting System (CBS) has been described as an "all-seeing eye," the presence of eyelids would indicate that, at some point, even this eye sleeps.

Although the eye can be understood as a protective symbol—the Egyptian *wedjat* "Eye of Horus," for instance—a fixed stare can be an aggressive act. Belief in the malevolent effects of the evil eye still persist in parts of the Mediterranean and Middle East, where eye-like symbols are used to negate its influence.

OPPOSITE
Under the Banner of Lenin for Socialist Construction, a 1930 photomontage propaganda poster by Latvian designer Gustav Klutsis. Six years after Lenin's death, Klutsis suggests that Stalin's vision for the Soviet Union is one with Lenin's.

2
If a third eye indicates an extension of vision that is extraordinary, then one eye belies a lesser vision—more nascent and bestial. French artist Odilon Redon explores this idea in his 1883 lithograph, *The Misshapen Polyp Floated on the Shores, a Sort of Smiling and Hideous Cyclops.*

3
"The eye (like the mouth) as a dream-image is often a veiled symbol for the female sexual orifice" [Biedermann]. Untitled screen print from the *Erotikon* series by American graphic designer Mark Fox (2009).

4
Voluntarily closing or covering one's eyes can be a sign of seeking access to an inner vision—and larger truths. (The Buddha is often depicted with his eyes closed, for example.) Ex libris for Mathilde Sanka by Slovak artist Karl Frech, c. 1920.

5
While sightlessness may symbolize judicial impartiality or love in the arts, in life impaired vision is generally equated with diminished circumstances. A peddler wears her handmade sign like a caption, presumably to evoke pity and generate income. *Blind,* by American photographer Paul Strand, 1916.

6
Until 2007 the tail fin of the Turkish airline Fly Air featured a traditional apotropaic symbol known as the *nazar bonjuk.* Popular in Mediterranean countries, the *nazar* is believed to ward off the evil eye; its use on an airplane would guarantee safe passage.

7

The oculus of the Pantheon in Rome, Italy. Dating from 126 CE, this architectural eye in the Pantheon's dome is a solar door, giving light entry into the temple's interior while simultaneously allowing access to the heavens above for those within the building.

8

A Japanese papier-mâché effigy of Bodhidharma, the Indian founder of Zen Buddhism. Known as *Daruma* in Japan, the effigies are bought with the eyes in a "blind" state. One eye is painted in (or symbolically opened) when a wish is made or a goal set; the second eye is painted if the wish is granted.

9

A Moroccan Berber talismanic design used to counter the evil eye. The central cross first draws then disperses the *djoun,* or evil forces, in the four cardinal directions.

10

Miniature figurines such as this are known as "eye idols" even though their original purpose is unclear. Their design varies, but one feature remains constant: a limbless torso with the head defined by outsize eyes. The five senses are elegantly reduced to one only: sight. Mesopotamia, Uruk period, c. 3500–3100 BCE.

MOUTH/TONGUE

As the organ of speech and breath, the mouth is the vehicle for creative utterances associated with generative power. The Egyptian god Ptah brings the world into being through language, as does the god of Genesis who declares, "Let there be light." The title of Russian poet Vladimir Mayakovsky's book of verse—*Dlia golosa,* or *For the Voice*—suggests that words become animate when voiced.

The mouth is also a symbol of expression and self-determination—freedom of speech is, to some degree, the freedom to open one's mouth. The scene from the Wachowski Brothers' 1999 science-fiction film *The Matrix,* in which the protagonist Neo has his mouth "erased" by Agent Smith, is a disturbing vision of forced silence. The Egyptian *Book of the Dead* includes the prayer, "Give me back my mouth, so that I may speak."

The open, omnivorous mouth can represent a door leading to death or to the underworld. A menacing mouth is a feature of devouring goddesses such as Kali, the Hindu goddess of death, as well as of Emma-O, the Japanese judge of the netherworld. Medieval depictions of the Gates of Hell commonly include infernal monsters who hold the damned in their gaping jaws. In the sacred architecture of Hinduism the *torana* gate represents Kali's open mouth: to pass through the gateway is to symbolically pass from life to death. (See *Door/Gate.*)

As sexual symbols, the mouth corresponds to the vulva, while the darting or protruding tongue has phallic significance. With the notable exception of Tibet, the extended tongue is considered a gesture of defiance or, as in Greek depictions of the Gorgon Medusa, of threat.

OPPOSITE
The Junkie, a 1971 Op-Ed piece for the *New York Times* by American illustrator Brad Holland. Like baby chicks clamoring to be fed, the junkie's multi-mouthed arm embodies the insatiable hunger of addiction. Interestingly, Holland's drawing was originally intended as a metaphor for welfare dependency.

2
With lips painted and parted, the female mouth is an icon of sexual desire associated with the vulva—although teeth cloud this correlation. Andy Warhol's portrait of Marilyn Monroe de-emphasizes the actress' teeth with color, enlarging her mouth in the process. *Untitled from Marilyn Monroe,* screenprint, 1967.

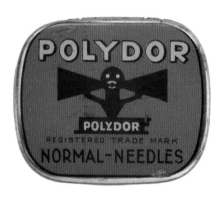

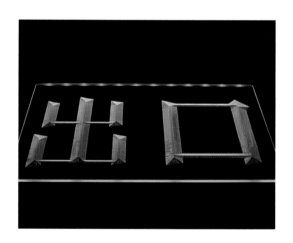

3
Kali—from *kala*, meaning time or destiny, as well as black—is the Hindu goddess of destruction, the great devourer. Kali's mouth marks the passage from life to death; her bloodred tongue, extended like a tentacle, signals her appetite for killing. India, late 19th or early 20th century, watercolor on paper. DETAIL

4
During the Han dynasty, jade cicadas known as tongue amulets were placed in the mouths of the dead to guard against evil. (As entry points, the mouth and other orifices were considered vulnerable.) The cicada is a Chinese symbol of cyclic rebirth and immortality. 206 BCE–220 CE.

5
The mouth literally gives voice to art in this trademark for German record company Polydor. The silhouette of two gramophone horns forms an X, the center of which corresponds with the mouth—the origin of song. Gramophone needle tin, c. 1925.

6
The Chinese words for "entrance" and "exit" are written with the pictograph for "mouth." Like the opening of a river or cave, the door is a metaphoric mouth, affording entrance to and exit from a building. The three-stroke character for "exit" frames a rectangular void on this contemporary sign.

7
Gary Panter's 1977 illustration
for Los Angeles punk band The
Screamers features a singer's
mouth that is simultaneously capable of both creative expression
and destructive menace. Italian
artist Fortunato Depero explores
a similar dualism in his *Futurist
Self-portrait* of 1915.

TEETH

Teeth, like hair, are symbols of power, vitality, and sexual potency. Strong, healthy teeth are associated with attack and defense; loose or broken teeth imply weakness. The loss of teeth generally signals a transition from one state to another: from child to adult or, in the case of adults, from maturity to infirmity. The loss of adult teeth marks the loss of youth and virility: to be "toothless" is to be impotent; to be "toothsome" is to be sexually attractive. (See *Hair.*)

"Etymologically, a *tooth* is an *eater*" [Ayto], and it is the machinery of our teeth that enables us to crush and assimilate food. Teeth are metaphoric millstones that, in their grinding action, symbolize change and fate. The menacing teeth of Kali, the Hindu goddess of destruction, emblematize the inexorable, transformative effects of time. (See *Mouth/Tongue.*)

Enameled, durable, and white, teeth are associated with bones, which are symbols of imperishable life force. The Greek myth of Cadmus sowing dragon's teeth to reap armed men is animated by the symbolism of the tooth as a "seed" with regenerative properties. Austrian neurologist Sigmund Freud linked dreams of aching or lost teeth with onanism, and in these contexts teeth are a proxy for semen.

To the Bambara of West Africa, the incisors—visible when one smiles with parted lips—are signs of fame and happiness; the sharp canines represent hard work or hatred; the molars are symbols of endurance or stubbornness. Among the ancient Maya, "upper incisors were sometimes filed to the T-shape of the sun god" [Miller and Taube] to mimic the appearance of the deity.

1

1

Ohaguro is the Japanese practice of blackening teeth that remained popular until the late 19th century. Its significance varied over hundreds of years, but teeth may have originally been blackened because they were associated with bone, which in Buddhist thought is considered unclean. (Contemporary Japanese women still cover their teeth with their hands when they laugh.) A Noh theater mask of a young woman of carved, lacquered, and painted wood; 18th–19th century, but based on a 14th-century design.

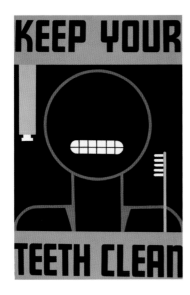

KEEP YOUR

TEETH CLEAN

lein-Plaka

Volkstänz

Orpheur

Irkund

2
"Keep Your Teeth Clean," a Federal Art Project poster intended to promote good public hygiene. Presumably inspecting his teeth in the mirror, this model US citizen's straight white teeth are a marker of his sound health. By an unidentified American designer, screen print, c. 1938.

3
A lowercase letter *s*, included in the word *Volkstänz*, from a specimen of the typeface Trump-Deutsch by German designer Georg Trump. The Roman letter *S* evolved from the Phoenician letter *sin* (or tooth), which is understood to represent two teeth. (The Greek letter *sigma* shares the same origin.) DETAIL

4
A serrated glyph of upper and lower incisors represents the action "to bite" in this rebus-based trademark for the advertising agency Man Bites Dog. While bared teeth are typically a sign of aggression, here the stylized teeth (and business name) represent an iconoclastic approach. By graphic designer Mark Fox, 1994.

5
The fear of being bitten is a primal one that is regularly exploited in films, among them *Nosferatu* (1922), *The Wolf Man* (1941), and in one horrifying scene, *Cape Fear* (1991). In *Dracula*, the vampire's lengthy canine teeth—fangs—indicate his predatory nature. Directed by Tod Browning, 1931.

FOOT/SHOE

The foot is a symbol of free will, freedom being expressed through mobility. Ostensibly predicated on an aesthetic or erotic ideal, the ancient Chinese practice of foot binding nonetheless resulted in a denial of autonomy for women.

Feet are essential to our stability and balance; a lame foot, therefore, can suggests weakness or imbalance. Dr. Strangelove, the wheelchair-bound former Nazi in Stanley Kubrick's 1964 eponymous film, exemplifies the folkloric association between physical defects and mental (or moral) defects. Medieval European depictions of demons frequently include nonhuman feet to indicate their evil nature; Satan, in particular, is envisioned as having webbed feet, talons, or cloven hooves.

The foot is the point of contact between our bodies and the earth, and this link to the material realm can impart the foot with negative associations. Originating with a dream of Nebuchadnezzar's, King of Babylon, to have "feet of clay" is to be prone to human weakness and fallibility.

In Islam the shoe is considered ritually unclean, and to be shown the sole of a shoe or have one flung at you is a sign of extreme contempt. When Iraqi cameraman Muntadar al-Zaidi threw his shoes at American President George W. Bush at a press conference in 2008—a "farewell kiss" to a "dog"—the symbolism was unequivocal.

In classical antiquity the shoe assumed the symbolism of liberty as slaves were forced to remain barefoot. The shoe thus acted as a marker of authority and of control.

OPPOSITE
Sixty pairs of iron shoes line the bank of the Danube in a memorial created by Hungarian artists Gyula Pauer and Can Togay (2005). Marking the execution of Budapest Jews at the river's edge by Arrow Cross fascists during WWII, the memorial also recalls the piles of discarded shoes at Nazi death camps.

2
The inner soles of these pharaonic sandals are decorated with bound captives—one Asian, one African—who represent two of Egypt's traditional nine enemies. The act of wearing the sandals symbolically subjugates the captives and confirms the wearer's authority. From the tomb of Tutankhamun, c. 1323 BCE.

3
In the ancient Levant, washing
the feet of a guest was a gesture
of hospitality and a display of
humility. In the painting *Saint
Mary Magdalen anointing the feet
of Christ*, Mary kneels on the floor
amidst discarded bones (and in
the company of a dog) to vener-
ate the Christ. Master of Perea,
Spain, c. 1500. DETAIL

4
Keep these off the U.S.A., a WWI propaganda poster designed by American illustrator John Norton in 1917. Prussian cavalry boots—note the spurs—are soaked in blood and marked with an imperial eagle to represent the rapaciousness of Germany under Kaiser Wilhelm II.

5
The exposed female foot is the only body part clearly silhouetted in this *shunga* woodblock print of two lovers. Toes clenched, the naked foot is an erotic cue for sexual ecstasy. Attributed to Japanese artist Katsukawa Shunsho, c. 18th century. DETAIL

6
American photojournalist Bill Gallagher's 1952 portrait of presidential candidate Adlai Stevenson revealed a hole in the sole of the politician's shoe. Keen to project a populist image, Stevenson's campaign produced sterling silver label pins to memorialize his Everyman shoe.

7
This limestone panel of the *Buddhapada*, or Buddha's footprints, may mark a locus of divine visitation. In some religious practices, footprints metaphorically indicate a particular spiritual path to follow. From the Great Stupa at Amaravati, India, 1st century BCE.

Twelfth Night

The Shakespeare Project *presents* Twelfth Night *or What You Will*, by Wm. Shakespeare. Admission is Free *Directed by* Scott Cargle. Our performances are; Central Park, Saturday June 11 at 12:00 PM and 4 PM. Sunday June 12 at 3:00 PM. Bryant Park, Sunday, June 19 and 26 at 3:00 PM. Fort Green Park, Brooklyn, Saturday, June 18 at 12:00 PM and 4:00 PM,. and at The Henry Street Settlement, Abrons Art Center, Thursday, June 16 at 6:00 PM. Donations are greatly appreciated.

HEART

The beating heart is physically and symbolically central to human life: it is the animate core, the hub of a network of arteries and veins that circulate blood throughout the body. It is likened to the sun around which the planets orbit, and is identified as a sacred point of contact between man and divinity, thus making it a spiritual locus as well.

Ancient Mesoamericans appear to have taken the metaphoric relationship between the heart and sun literally. Believing that the sun fed on human hearts, the Aztecs practiced heart extrusion on live captives; the Incas likewise sacrificed llamas while the animals faced east, offering the sun their hearts and blood. (See *Sun.*)

While understood as a symbol of love, compassion, and courage in the Occident, in older traditions the heart is believed to be the seat of intuitive knowledge rather than of emotions. In Islam and Hinduism the phrase "the eye of the heart" expresses the idea that the heart is an organ of perception and thus illumination. In Chinese, the word for "mind" is written with characters that literally mean "thoughts of the heart."

As metaphoric equivalents, the heart may be represented by a sun, lotus, or diamond. The heart may also take the form of an inverted triangle, which associates it with water, rain, female sexuality, and fecundity. An icon of a red heart generally evokes love, romance, compassion, or mercy; the black heart may suggest loathing, dispassion, or mourning. The inverted heart, point up, may assume the symbolism of the phallic spade. (See *Triangle.*)

2

OPPOSITE
In the Occident the heart is considered the seat of emotions and, in particular, of desire. American designer James Victore playfully equates the heart with another locus of desire on this 1993 poster for a performance of William Shakespeare's comedy *Twelfth Night, or What You Will.*

2
In ancient Egypt the heart was judged by Osiris after death. As the storehouse of memory, however, there was a risk that the heart might divulge a lifetime of misdeeds. To prevent this fate the mummy was equipped with a substitute heart amulet guaranteed to vouch for the dead. Opaque glass, c. 1479–1292 BCE.

3
One of a system of sociopolitical icons for the activist phone company Credo Mobile. Two interlaced hearts—symmetrical and balanced—symbolize the issue of Marriage Equality. Same-sex marriage was finally legalized in the United States by the Supreme Court in 2015. Designed by Mark Fox and Angie Wang, 2013.

4
The central, heart-shaped cutout on this child's chair is not merely decorative. In a kind of creative ensoulment, American industrial designers Charles and Ray Eames animate the form by endowing it with a heart and thus life. Molded plywood, c. 1945.

5
A mosaic floor replete with life symbolism: the swastika is solar; the cross is the fertile union of opposites; the heart is a life center. The octagon surrounding each heart evokes the number eight, which is associated with renewal and spiritual rebirth. Lullingstone Roman Villa, Kent, England, c. 100 CE. DETAIL

6
In Hindu, Islamic, and Jewish thought the heart is the abode or temple of gods, which we carry within ourselves. To confirm his honorable intentions to the goddess Sita, Hanuman reveals that her husband Rama and his brother Lakshmana "dwell" within his heart. Pigment on paper, Calcutta, India, c. 1880.

HAIR

Hair is a symbol of power, vitality, and virility, and it shares some of the meanings of the radiating nimbus. (Hair is symbolically connected to the sun's rays.) The North American Indian practice of scalping—removing an enemy's scalp with its hair intact—ritualistically "steals" an enemy's power and vital life force. It is a kind of castration. (See *Nimbus*.)

Head hair is associated with the intellect and its creative energies; other body hair is linked with the physical self and its procreative and destructive potentialities. A covering of body hair suggests bestial tendencies. (See *Ape/Monkey*.)

In the Occident, long hair on men has historically signified noble lineage (France), freeborn status (Germany), or political liberty. The Romans referred to the territory of independent Gaul as *Gallia Comata,* or Hairy Gaul, to distinguish its long-haired inhabitants from those Gauls under Roman occupation.

The forced cutting of hair typically accompanies a fundamental change in status for an individual. For military conscripts, convicts, and religious initiates, it marks a denial of the individual self, a loss of personal freedom, and a requisite submission to higher authority. French female collaborators were publicly humiliated with forced head shavings at the conclusion of WWII as a way to mark women whose sexual relations with German soldiers were considered odious. For men and women who suffer hair loss following illness or chemotherapy, the absence of hair is a potent symbol of their mortality.

OPPOSITE
A Christ-like figure appeals to Germany's women to sacrifice their hair for the manufacture of drive belts at the close of WWI. Long hair was seen as an integral feature of female identity; cutting it represented a weakening or loss of that identity. Illustration by German poster artist Jupp Wiertz, 1918. DETAIL

2
For more than 200 years the ruling Manchus forced Han Chinese men to adopt the hairstyle known as the Manchu queue (French for tail). Refusal to adopt the queue was punishable by death; as a result, the queue functioned as a Qing Dynasty symbol of subjugation. A Chinese man in San Francisco's Chinatown, c. 1910.

3

Until the first half of the 20th century, unmarried Hopi girls wore their hair in distinctive whorls to signify their single status; married Hopi women wore their hair in braids. American photographer Edward S. Curtis recorded this portrait of Chaiwa, a Tewa girl, around 1906.

4

The plaited hair in this Victorian mourning brooch (c. 1850) resists decay and so symbolizes the fixity of the living soul. This theme is reinforced: gold conveys incorruptibility, the fretted border repeats endlessly, and the interwoven strands of hair suggest an eternal, unbreakable bond.

5

Crowning the head, hair is a symbol of power—all the more when that hair is comprised of snakes. The Gorgon Medusa would prove far less horrific were it not for her animate hair. *The Head of Medusa* by Belgian painter Peter Paul Rubens, c. 1618. DETAIL

6

Billowing hair issues from the head of Bob Dylan in American designer Milton Glaser's 1967 portrait of the artist. The multicolored spirals of Dylan's hair are a visible sign of his creative life force and echo the unruly hair of the Hindu deity Shiva. (Shiva's hair is the source of the river Ganges, a symbol of fecundity.)

NIMBUS

A nimbus is a luminous vapor, a "cloud" of light
that emanates from the head or body. Likely
derived from the sun and its radiance, the nimbus
is an attribute of sky and sun gods and signifies
supreme power, supernatural status, or holiness.
(See *Sun.*)

The nimbus occurs in both Oriental and Occidental iconography. Images of Buddha and Shiva
may include a nimbus, as may portraits of Helios,
Apollo, and deified Roman emperors. In Byzantine and Roman Catholic Christian iconography
the nimbus is conventionally depicted as a disk
centered immediately behind the head—a halo.
(From the Greek, *halos* means threshing floor: a
flat, circular area paved with stones.) When the
nimbus fully encloses the figure its shape is typically ovoid. This almond silhouette (*mandorla*
in Italian) suggests a flame, passage, or vulva,
and frequently appears in representations of the
Virgin Mary.

Corona in Latin, the crown encircles the head like
the aura surrounding the sun or moon and may
be considered a man-made nimbus. Whether the
crown is of gold or of leaves (as on a wreath) the
effect is the same: it honors the head, which is the
seat of wisdom and a symbol of one's life-force.

The European ruff collar of the 16th and 17th
centuries functions as a kind of sartorial nimbus. Elaborate Tudor ruffs such as those worn
by Queen Elizabeth I radiate out from the neck,
silhouetting the head against a luxurious spray of
linen and lace.

1

1

*Give in the Struggle Against
Hunger and Cold:* designer
Ludwig Hohlwein personifies the
German nation in this 1933 winter
relief poster. Stripped to the waist
and with one gold coin forming
a stigma, Hohlwein's figure
intentionally evokes the pathos of
the crucified Christ. The Nazi flag
"halo" denotes divinity.

2

Created to mark America's entry into WWI, this 1917 poster depicts the American eagle crowning the British lion with a wreath of victory. A crown of leaves—like the nimbus—encircles the head and glorifies the wearer. *America's Tribute to Britain,* by American illustrator F.G. Cooper. DETAIL

3

The eagle is a solar bird whose feathers represented the sun's rays to the Plains Indians of North America. A headdress of eagle feathers thus symbolically radiates light. Portrait of Three Horses by American photographer Edward S. Curtis, c. 1905.

4

A contemporary Mexican icon of Our Lady of Guadalupe, carved in wood and encircled with *milagros.* The nimbus enveloping Mary's entire body is generally almond-shaped, and the origins of its orificial silhouette may allude to the Roman Catholic doctrine of the virgin birth.

5

Designed by French sculptor Frédéric-Auguste Bartholdi, the statue of *Liberty Enlightening the World* is a monument to freedom; the rays of light projecting from Liberty's crown represent Earth's seven continents. The head of the statue on display in a Parisian park, by French photographer Albert Fernique (1883).

TWINS

Twins are inherently dualistic, and this dualism can be manifested as an oppositional force or as a complementary one. When in conflict, twins can represent the tension between mind and body, day and night, or life and death. The fratricidal twins Romulus and Remus and the rival twins Jacob and Esau exemplify brothers at enmity.

When twins are not oppositional their strengths are exponentially increased. This additive aspect is reflected in the related word "twine": a string that is strengthened by coiling a second strand around it. This symbolism is common in heraldic designs featuring a pair of like animals, such as two addorsed lions. The two towers of an Egyptian pylon, a pair of obelisks, and New York's Twin Towers can all be understood as monumental twins with mutually magnifying strengths.

In parts of Africa and in ancient China, twins were seen as unnatural and considered an ill omen. The Bantu put twins to death; the Chinese thought of mixed-sex twins as a "ghostly couple" and might put one or both to death. That identical twins are, in some sense, simultaneously singular and multiple perplexes even contemporary cultures. American photographer Diane Arbus' 1967 portrait of twin girls in Roselle, New Jersey, captures the visual oddity of seemingly mirror images that do not mirror. Arbus was renown for photographing what she termed "freaks."

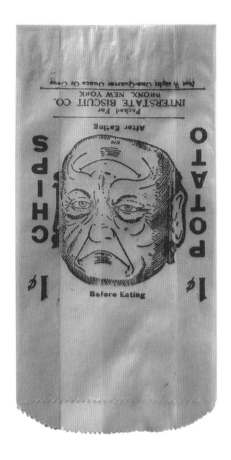

OPPOSITE
The Political Janus: It All Depends on the Way You Look at Him, an illustration by Australian satirist Frank A. Nankivell for *Puck* magazine, 1910. Former American President Theodore Roosevelt is rendered as a polarizing political figure, a simultaneous "savior" and "menace." DETAIL

2
Our dual nature is alluded to by the design of this potato-chip bag for the Interstate Biscuit Company, c. 1920. No doubt intended to amuse, it nonetheless expresses our capacity for happiness and sadness, as well as for good and evil. Like Dr. Jekyll and Mr. Hyde, this twin only reveals one face at a time.

3
From 1915 to 1919, the two-man German graphic design studio Wilhelmwerk identified itself with the sign for Gemini, which denotes the twins Castor and Pollux. Similar to the Roman numeral II, the mark implies "the joining of two souls, one intuitive, one rational, in order to achieve greater creativity" [Fontana].

4
The Roman god Janus can be seen as a pair of twins, with one of his faces looking forward to the future and the second face looking back to the past. Calendar printers Liebes & Teichtner are the two faces of Janus, namesake of January, on this poster stamp designed by Viennese artist Leon Lico Amar around 1913.

5
The J.A. Henckels *Zwilling* (or Twin) trademark has been in use since 1731, although the version that appears on this Friodur straight razor was likely designed by Wilhelmwerk around 1917. The twins' linked arms look as if they were constructed from a manual crank handle—the visual effect is one of unified effort.

6
The Twin Towers in Manhattan, New York, designed by American architect Minoru Yamasaki in the 1960s. At a height of 110 stories, these monumental twins were the tallest buildings in the world at their completion in 1971. Conceived of and built as a pair, the towers were likewise destroyed in tandem.

WHEEL
ARROW/BOW
HAMMER
DOOR/GATE
CITY
CHAIR/THRONE
MIRROR
BREAD
BOOK
AIRPLANE

man-made

WHEEL

The rotating wheel is an Occidental symbol of sequential states, including cycles of being (life and death) and of time (past, present, future). The ceaseless revolutions of the medieval Wheel of Fortune typify life's instability and ephemerality. In Tibetan Buddhism the wheel's rotations are a metaphor for the repetitious existence created by the material world and its illusions. Those who cling to this wheel are destined to suffer through endless cycles of life, death, and rebirth.

The potter's wheel and spinning wheel are both associated with life and its origins. In ancient Egyptian myth, animals, humans, and even gods were moulded from clay on the potter's wheel of the god Khnemu; in Greek thought it was the three Fates who spun the thread of each human life, measuring out its length. The spinning of a wheel is inherent in these acts of creation, and mirrors the rotary action of the cosmos: the orbiting of the planets, the revolutions of the stars, and the apparent arc of the sun across the heavens.

Associated with martial conquest, the chariot wheel is a dynamic sign of kingship and diety. (That a spoked wheel can also be seen as a sun with rays of light emanating from its center only adds to its potency.) Early Anatolian chariots had wheels with four spokes, and Mycenaean Greeks used the four-spoked wheel as a Linear B glyph to represent the syllable *ka;* in the Phoenician writing system it is known as *teth,* or wheel. The four-spoked wheel can also suggest the world and its four quarters; the Indian eight-spoked wheel may allude to the eight-petaled lotus. (See *Sun.*)

1
La Roue de Fortune, or Wheel of Fortune, the tenth card of the Major Arcana in a tarot deck. Illustrating a journey that leads nowhere, the Wheel of Fortune represents the constantly chang-ing—and ultimately futile—nature of existence. From the Marseille tarot published by B.P. Grimaud, France, c. 1930.

2
Like a ship's wheel, the automo-bile steering wheel is a nexus of control and thus agency. (It is the symbolic opposite of the Wheel of Fortune.) The symmetrical de-sign of this trademark reinforces its evocation of stability. For Kraft Versicherungs, an insurer of automobile clubs, by German designer Karl Schulpig, 1923.

3

The breaking wheel was employed as a medieval instrument of public torture and execution. Also called the Catherine Wheel after accounts of Catherine of Alexandria's martyrdom, the wheel is a Catholic emblem of religious fidelity. A Greek icon of the 4th-century saint by Dutch painter Jan Victors, 17th century.

4

A trademark for German steelmaker A. Borsig, designed by Wilhelm Deffke in 1917. This corporate "coat of arms" swaps out the typical heraldic shield for a steam-powered locomotive wheel. Here the wheel is primarily a symbol of industry, but its four-spoked form nonetheless evokes the neolithic German sun cross.

5

While the advent of the wheel and axle were exploited in the Near East as innovations for waging war, the wheel's significance to pre-Columbian Mesoamerica is unclear. The use of the wheel and axle appears to have been limited to small ceramic figurines like this dog. Mexico, Veracruz, 450–650 CE.

6

Mohandas Gandhi in the company of his spinning wheel, or *charkha*, photographed by Margaret Bourke-White in 1946. To foster economic and political independence, Gandhi implored "every Indian to spin his own cotton and weave his own cloth." The *charkha* is thus equated with Indian self-determination.

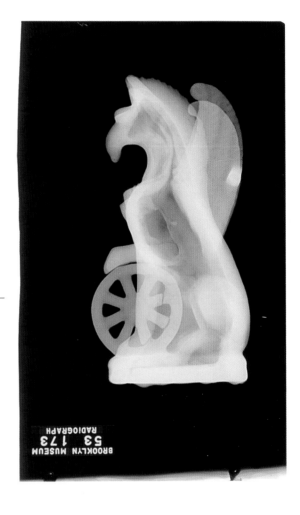

7
A Shinglay Lama turns a giant prayer wheel in the former kingdom of Sikkim. The spinning of the wheel activates Buddhist mantras, animating the wheel's prayers as if the words were spoken aloud. The rotating prayer wheel enlivens like a metaphoric sun. Photographed by Dr. Alice S. Kandell, 1965–71.

8
Nemesis takes the form of a winged, female griffin in this radiograph of a faience statuette. The Greek goddess of divine retribution, Nemesis rests her right paw on an eight-spoked wheel to signal her control over it; the wheel itself is a symbol of man's inescapable fate. Roman Egypt, 2nd century CE.

9
A universal message: *Amsterdam Loves Bikes*. The bicycle is not merely a mode of transportation for the Dutch—it represents an approach to urban living that values simplicity and modesty. The bicycle, literally "two wheels," connotes liberty as well: freedom of movement, yes, but also freedom *from* the polluting internal combustion engine. Designed for the City of Amsterdam by Dsgnfrm and Razormind, 2009.

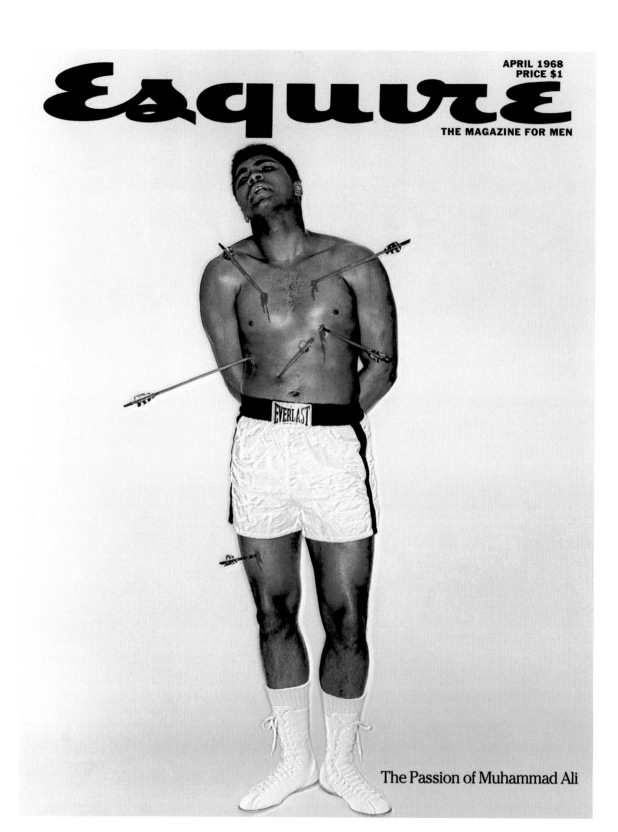

APRIL 1968
PRICE $1

Esquire

THE MAGAZINE FOR MEN

The Passion of Muhammad Ali

ARROW/BOW

Attributes of the hunter and warrior, the arrow and bow are marks of authority—including the authority to take life. The arrow is a symbol of speed, martial power, sudden death, and once released from the bow, irrevocable action. As emblems of the Greek sun god Apollo and the Hindu sky god Indra, arrows are rays of sunlight; when likened to the penetrating phallus or fertilizing rain the arrow is a symbol of male sexuality and of life. (See *Sun; Water.*)

The Hindu god of love, Kama, wields a sugarcane bow with a bowstring of bees: love is sweet, but it can sting. His piercing arrows induce longing but, unlike those of Eros, Kama's arrows are tipped with flowers. While blossom arrowheads suggest fecundity, their ephemerality may foreshadow the transience of desire. (See *Flower.*)

French poster artist A.M. Cassandre's personal trademark depicts a man caught mid-stride by an arrow shot through his right eye. The arrow represents the visual impact of Cassandre's work and crystallizes the observation that "The poster is an optic scandal" [Rossi]. An arrow piercing the eye is a Buddhist motif as well, and expresses the concept of sensory stimuli impinging on our consciousness whether we welcome it or not.

In modern iconographic usage, the arrow is used as a directional device: it points, or suggests movement. In right-reading countries the right-facing arrow suggests future or progress; the left-facing arrow indicates past or regress. The Hungarian Arrow Cross—an equilateral cross with each arm terminated by an arrowhead—is a fascist symbol of continuous outward expansion and dominance. (See *Cross.*)

OPPOSITE
A 1968 *Esquire* magazine cover by American art director George Lois. Modeled on Christian martyr St. Sebastian, world heavyweight champion Muhammad Ali is mock-executed for his refusal to renounce his stance as a Black Muslim and fight in the Vietnam war. The arrows symbolize the boxer's public condemnation.

2
Bound arrows suggest strength in unity—an idea also shared by the Roman *fasces,* a bundle of wooden rods surmounted by an axe head. (Broken arrows, by contrast, symbolized peace among Native Americans.) Trademark for an unknown company by German designer Walter Sauer, 20th century.

3
The union of the male, solar
arrow with the female, lunate
bow evokes fertility and hence
offspring. In this trademark for
Robert Stevens Photography, the
procreative symbolism becomes
a metaphor for the creative
act of making photographs. By
American graphic designer Mark
Fox, 1998.

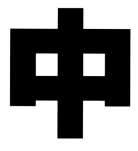

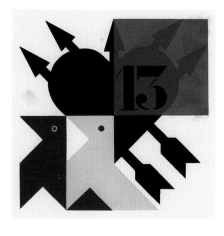

4

The bow is an ancient symbol of war and the authority to wage it. The Mamluk sultan's *Bunduqdar,* or Keeper of the Bow, is represented on this lamp by an emblem of two mirrored bows. The doubling of the form magnifies the weapon's symbolic power. Gilded and enameled glass, Cairo, Egypt, after 1285.

5

The Chinese character *zhong,* meaning center, depicts an arrow bisecting a square target. As the Chinese refer to their country as *Zhongguo,* or Middle Kingdom, the idea of centrality—as well as of a single arrow striking the bull's-eye perfectly—is embedded in the Chinese conception of their national identity.

6

Ex Libris of Baron Philippe de Rothschild by French designer Jean Carlu, around 1928. Adapted from a motif in the family crest, the five arrows represent the five sons of patriarch Mayer Rothschild, each of whom founded a banking house. That the arrows are collectively piercing one heart is a sign of their unity.

7

Used as fletching, bird feathers imbue the arrow with ascensional symbolism that links the archer with the heavens. This feather surcoat may function in a similar manner, perhaps even offering divine protection to the samurai who wore it. The significance of the feathered target motif is unclear. Japan, 16th century.

HAMMER

Both tool and weapon, the hammer embodies the oppositional acts of creation and destruction. The hammer can be used to drive a nail or carve a letterform in stone, or it can be directed to crush the skulls of enemies on the battlefield. This dualism is reflected in the double-hammer of the Norse sky god, Thor. Named *Mjölnir,* "The Grinder" or "The Crusher," Thor's hammer levels mountains but can also reanimate the dead. Miniature renditions of Thor's hammer—called *torshammere*—were worn as protective amulets by Vikings during the 10th century.

Wielded by the Greco-Roman smithies Hephaestus and Vulcan to fashion thunderbolts for the sky god, the hammer is a proxy for the bolt itself—a phallic, procreative force associated with the fertilizing properties of rain. The relationship between hammer and anvil—reminiscent of male/female productivity—is also echoed in the pairing of the hammer and chisel. According to Chinese creation myths from the 3rd to 6th centuries, the world was given its form by P'an Ku, the first being and only offspring of *yin* and *yang.* P'an Ku shapes the cosmos out of primordial chaos with his hammer and chisel. (See *Lightning.*)

Traditionally associated with craft and the mythic arts of creation, by the 20th century the hammer came to signify the mechanistic nature of industrial labor. This symbolism finds expression in the familiar Communist hammer-and-sickle, as well as in the work of Italian artist Fortunato Depero, whose *Machine Hammerers* of 1925 features a phalanx of mallet-wielding automatons.

The striking of the hammer can signal resolution or a moment of reckoning: the clock's hammer sounding a bell on the hour, or the hammering of the judge's gavel to return a courtroom to order.

1

1

"Sive Iconoclasts," a poster designed for the 1995 San Francisco Museum of Modern Art Design Lecture Series by American graphic designer Mark Fox. The five speakers—all *eikonoklastes,* or image destroyers—are symbolized by the eye and crossed hammers. The image is juxtaposed with a quote attributed to Russian poet Vladimir Mayakovsky that posits a muscular role for the arts: "Art is not a mirror to reflect the world, but a hammer with which to shape it." Offset lithography.

2

Representing the union of urban laborers and rural peasants, the hammer-and-sickle was adopted as an emblem of Communist Russia in 1923. Its use on a trinket as banal as this glass Christmas ornament is a testament to the pervasiveness of Soviet propaganda. Ukraine, 1960s.

3

Signifying the flourishing of industry, a hammer rises from the fertile German soil as naturally as a flowering plant a mere three and a half years after the nation's defeat in WWI. A poster stamp for a 1922 German Trade Show held in Munich by designer René Binder.

4

A silver ring with an ansated (or looped) tau cross, a symbol of St. Anthony likely derived from the Egyptian ankh. To the Vikings, the tau cross depicted Thor's double-hammer, a symbol of the thunderbolt linked with rain, fertility, and good luck. Its function on a ring is apotropaic. Germany, 1400–1500.

5

A photograph of US Senator Sam Ervin (center), Chairman of the Senate Watergate Committee, conferring with colleagues during the 1973 investigation into Richard Nixon's reelection for President. The senator's gavel—a gift from the Cherokee nation and symbol of his authority to lead—rests before him.

DOOR/GATE

The potential entrance to—or exit from—a designated space, the door is a point of control and, therefore, power. Its specific symbolism is largely dependent on its state: closed or open, locked or unlocked, guarded or unguarded. In general, the door and gate function as symbols of access, transition, transformation, birth, and rebirth.

As a symbol of time the door constitutes the threshold of the present, separating past from future. One notable metaphoric door in the Gregorian calendar is midnight on December 31, New Year's Eve. The name of the first month of the new year, January, stems from the Latin *janua* (door), and is associated with Janus, the Roman god of thresholds and beginnings. (See *Twins*.)

To dispel evil and invite good luck, doorways may be protected with auspicious symbols. Arrangements of evergreen boughs—*kadomatsu* (gate pine)—are traditionally placed at the entrance to Japanese homes to attract favor for the new year. (This practice is now virtual: a *kadomatsu* emoji is available on social media.) Among Moroccan Berbers, the body's orifices are akin to doors through which evil might enter if left unprotected. As a result, Berber women, in particular, may be tattooed on the nose, on the lower lip and chin, between the eyes, and on the pubis. The tattoos are apotropaic and serve to safeguard the body.

Like a book, the open door suggests access to knowledge and release from (mental or physical) confinement; the closed or locked door limits knowledge. In Chinese thought the opening and closing of the door is likened to the endless push-and-pull of *yin* and *yang* forces. In this context the door is the dynamic boundary between complementary opposites. (See *Book*.)

OPPOSITE
The Porte Monumentale by French architect René Binet for the 1900 Paris World Exposition. Inspired by the skeletal remains of microscopic protozoa, Binet's design revels in the new vision wrought by scientific innovation. The gate is a portal to the new century that leads from past to future, ignorance to knowledge.

2
The door is a protective barrier that elicits the concept of maternal sheltering; it can also represent a forbidden threshold that is best left uncrossed. In American director Stanley Kubrick's 1980 horror film *The Shining,* a violently breached door parallels the dissolution of the writer Jack Torrance's mind.

3

Conceived as an 18th-century symbol of peace, Berlin's Brandenburg Gate would later serve as a triumphal arch for a succession of French, Prussian, and Nazi troops. With the closing of East Berlin's borders in 1961, the inaccessible Gate epitomized the loss of freedoms under communist rule.

4

The origin of the Roman letter *D* is the Egyptian hieroglyph *dalt,* or door. It was drawn with the door in a horizontal position, its pins projecting from the upper corners. (The Hebrew letter *dalet* evolved from the hieroglyph as well.) The typeface Oblong by Dutch designers René Knip and Janno Hahn, 2012.

5

The Japanese *torii* marks the entrance to Shinto shrines or venerated sites. It delineates the approach to sacred space, but cannot bar entry. Always "open," the *torii*'s design suggests that, in Shinto thought, access to the divine should be unfettered. The Itsukushima shrine on the Seto inland sea, Japan, 16th century.

6

The split gate in Balinese architecture may reference "the two halves of Mount Meru severed by Siva to invite passage" [Geertz]. This lintel-less doorway at Pura Lempuyang in Bali, Indonesia, frames the sky without boxing it; the tapering masonry leads the eye upward, beyond the limits of the terrestrial.

CITY

In contrast to a nomadic camp or the haphazard arrangement of individual dwellings, the city comprises a community within a fixed, demarcated space that incorporates both private and public architecture. The sense of fixity may be reinforced by the city's design: square or rectangular plans, common to Roman colonies, suggest immutability and permanence. (See *Square*.)

Like a castle or citadel, the city—especially one that is walled—can be understood as a protective enclosure with maternal significance. While this association with the female sex is nearly always positive, the early Christian characterization of Rome as the whore of Babylon, "drunk with blood," is a notable exception. The symbolism of the city as a nurturing mother is now inverted, its narrative shifted from life to death.

As a hub of learning, the city represents sophistication and taste, "urban" and "urbane" sharing the same Latin root. To enter the city is to trigger "the process of civilization; to become urban [is] to 'citizenize' the person" [Turner and Hamilton]. French philosopher Jean-Jacques Rousseau credits urbanites themselves for any civilizing transformation, insisting that "houses make a town, but citizens [make] a city."

When civil society yields to uncivil behavior, the city can emblematize ethical or moral decay. The names of the Biblical cities Sodom and Gomorrah, destroyed by an act of divine wrath, have become bywords for licentiousness. Las Vegas, Nevada—proudly known as Sin City—monetizes its reputation for consequence-free vice by marketing itself to tourists with the slogan, "What happens in Vegas, stays in Vegas."

OPPOSITE
The verticality of the city of the future is emphasized by the proportions of this film poster by Heinz Schulz-Neudamm (1926). A female automaton appears to carry the city on her shoulders—a visual cue for the unseen workers who toil below ground for the profit of others above. *Metropolis,* by German director Fritz Lang.

2
The Syrian city of Dura-Europos personified as Atargatis, its tutelary deity. Like the Greco-Roman goddesses of chance, Tyche and Fortuna, Atargatis wears a crown of crenellated walls to indicate her role as urban protectress. Bas-relief limestone sculpture, 1st century CE.

3
One of the distinguishing
features of city life is a pace
governed by increasingly smaller
increments of time: the hour,
minute, second, and—in the case
of high-frequency stock trading
on Wall Street—millisecond.
Tempo of the City: I by American
photographer Berenice Abbott.
Gelatin silver print, 1938.

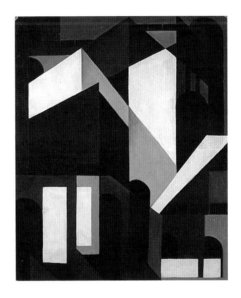

4

The form of the Roman letter *B* is ultimately derived from the Egyptian hieroglyph for "house." All that remains of the original glyph—a linear ground plan—is the sense of an enclosed space. A calligraphy nibs manual by Heintze & Blanckertz, with lettering by Prof. Wilhelm Krause. Germany, 1928.

5

American Precisionist Louis Lozowick reduces the urban environment to a series of geometric planes to examine the constructed nature of the modern city. While the house may indeed be a "machine" for living, this monochromatic city is rendered as a machine for production. *City Shapes,* oil on board, 1922–23.

6

The Aztec equivalent of the English "temple" is *teocalli,* or god house, and for Mesoamericans the temple served as a point of contact between humans and the divine. Befitting its civic import, the temple was generally erected at the city center. Mezcala temple model, Mexico, carved stone, 300 BCE–500 CE.

7

A *tulou* or earthen building in Fujian Province, China, designed to house—and protect—an entire clan. Some *tulou* rise four stories and can accommodate 100 families, their diameter spanning nearly a tenth of a mile. In this context, the extended family constitutes a city unto itself.

CHAIR/THRONE

The chair elevates us, both literally and figuratively. Held aloft, midway between standing and squatting, the chair removes us from the ground and so from the company of beasts. To sit in a chair is to ascend the evolutionary ladder—or at least one rung of it.

The throne may be considered a sacred point of contact between man and the divine, an *axis mundi* activated by the presence of the sovereign. For example, the 16th-century Aztec stone throne was inscribed with two symbolic motifs: the earth monster on the seat and a rayed sun on the backrest. The bridging of earth and sky—of the terrestrial and celestial—could only be accomplished if Motecuhzoma II was physically seated on his throne. In related symbolism, the pronouncements of the Roman Catholic pope are considered infallible when spoken *ex cathedra,* or from the throne.

The chair and throne are oddly human, comprising legs, arms, a seat, and back. "The original throne is the lap of the Great Mother" [Ronnberg and Martin], and in ancient Egypt the goddess Isis embodied the king's throne. As every living pharaoh was equated with Horus, the son of Isis, when an Egyptian monarch sat on his throne he sat in the lap of his mother. The parallels between the embrace of a comfortable chair and that of a comforting parent likely inform the chair's anthropomorphic symbolism.

A poster featuring American political activist Huey P. Newton, the Black Panther Party's "Minister of Defence" [sic]. The chair's expansive, ovoid back creates a wicker halo that transform's the young activist into a leather-clad saint for the Black Power movement. The pose might be dismissed as mere theater if it weren't for the shotgun shells scattered at Newton's feet—and for the warning, in small print, to "The racist dog policemen." Photography attributed to Blair Stapp; composition by Eldridge Cleaver. Offset lithography, 1967.

2
A Bamileke or Bamum stool, intended for ceremonial display as an expression of royal power. The leopard caryatid—a "king" of beasts and notably danger- ous—lends figurative and literal support to the king's rule. The beadwork and cowrie shells proclaim the king's prestige. Cameroon, 19th–20th century.

3
"Furniture of our Times," a poster for the Herman Miller Collec- tion by Swiss designer Armin Hofmann. Ten nested chair seats hover in space, unmoored from their legs as well as from the floor. Reduced to pure silhouette, their forms function as icons of modern furniture design. Linocut and letterpress, 1962.

4
A Europeanized portrait of Huayna Capac, the twelfth Inca king. Painted approximately two hundred years after his death in 1525, this image is likely more mythic than literal. The throne's arms wrap around Huayna Capac in a protective embrace, but the king appears oddly constrained. Peru, possibly mid-18th century.

5
The electric chair at Auburn State Prison, New York, c. 1908. As a restraining device this chair is designed less for the condemned and more for the convenience of the executioner. Artist Andy War- hol used the chair from Sing Sing prison as an icon of American culture in his *Death and Disaster* series, beginning in 1963.

MIRROR

Due to its reflective properties, the mirror is closely associated with light, clarity, truth, and knowledge. Circular mirrors, in particular, can suggest the dome of the sky or the radiance of the sun or full moon. In Japan, the mirror is a symbol of the sun goddess Amaterasu; ancient Egyptian mirrors generally feature a polished disc of bronze or copper alloy that likely represents the sun. (See *Sun; Moon.*)

In Hindu and Buddhist thought, the mirror isn't a symbol of truth but of illusion as it merely replicates the world of appearances—which is itself illusory. Tellingly, the English words "mirror" and "mirage" share the same Latin root: *mirari,* meaning "to wonder at." To gaze into a mirror is to gape at a mirage.

The mirrored surface—whether a pool of water, a polished stone or metal disc, or the jaguar's eyes—can be understood as a portal to another realm, or as a passage to occult knowledge. (The plot of English author Lewis Carroll's 1871 novel *Through the Looking-Glass and What Alice Found There* is premised on a mirror-as-door.) Ancient Mesoamericans used a range of polished stones as divinatory mirrors, including iron pyrite and the black volcanic glass obsidian. Razor-sharp when given an edge, obsidian is highly symbolic as a material as it was used for both ritual bloodletting (when a blade) and necromancy (when used as a mirror). Olmec stone mirrors are concave and thus capable of igniting fire—a feature that would reinforce the mirror's solar symbolism. (See *Water; Eye; Door/Gate; Fire.*)

2

OPPOSITE
Washington, D.C. Negro woman in her bedroom, a portrait by American photographer Gordon Parks, 1942. French philosopher Michel Foucault identifies the mirror as a heterotopia, "a place without a place." The reflected image constitutes an alternate reality—a space we can see, but cannot enter.

2
A mosaic-covered human skull thought to represent the omnipotent Aztec deity Tezcatlipoca, or Smoking Mirror. Polished pyrite mirrors—used for divination in Mesoamerica—protrude from the skull's eye sockets to signal that this god can "see" the future. Mixtec/Aztec, turquoise, lignite, and shell, c. 1400–1521.

3
In Japanese legend, the mirror
is inherently magical and prone
to revealing hidden truths—in
this case, that a warlord's son is a
practitioner of rat sorcery. *Shu-
mitsu Kanja Yoshitaka Reflecting
as a Rat in a Mirror,* a woodblock
print by Japanese artist Tsukioka
Yoshitoshi (1867). DETAIL

4
The mirror is a medieval cue for narcissism frequently found in the hand of Luxuria, the personification of vanity and lust. The modern equivalent of Luxuria's mirror is the smartphone and its kin, the selfie. American President Barack Obama gamely promoting the website HealthCare.gov in 2015.

5
Beyond their utilitarian function, small, round mirrors were used as protective amulets in ancient China. Polished metal mirrors were positioned in bedrooms and worn by brides to deflect the influence of evil spirits. The back of a cast bronze mirror with an eight-pointed star, China, Eastern Han dynasty, 25–220 CE.

6
The symbol for the female sex—as well as for the planet Venus and element copper—is derived from the mirror held by the Greco-Roman goddesses of love. The copper and bronze mirrors of the ancient Near East tend to conform to this prototypical design. Woodcut by Rudolf Koch and Fritz Kredel, 1923.

7
The climactic hall of mirrors scene from American director Orson Welles' 1948 film noir *The Lady from Shanghai*. Multiple mirrors create a sense of spatial disorientation that corresponds to the illusory nature of Michael and Elsa's relationship. The truth becomes apparent only with the shattering of the mirrors.

BREAD

Bread is such a basic necessity in the Occident that it is equated with life itself. To have bread is to have life; not having bread is tantamount to death. (The analogous staple throughout Asia is rice; bread was unknown in Japan until its introduction by Portuguese missionaries in the 16th century.)

Leavened bread is a symbol of transformation, the end product of a mysterious—if not miraculous—process that turns what is essentially a grass into a sustaining meal. American food writer Michael Pollan describes the Neolithic invention (or discovery) of leavened bread in his 2013 book *Cooked* as a "technology for transforming nature into nourishment." The collective labor represented by a loaf of bread—entailing planting, harvesting, milling, and baking—suggests that bread has served as an engine of cultural transformation as well. (See *Fire*.)

Made from the flour of countless individual grains, a loaf of bread is a manifestation of coalescence. This significance is deepened when bread is "broken": derived from the Latin *panis* or bread, one's "companion" is literally the one with whom you share your bread. (This symbolism is embedded in the Christian sacrament of Communion.)

Like seed within a fruit, ears of wheat are sexual and fertility symbols associated with the Phrygian earth goddess Cybele and the Greco-Roman goddesses Demeter and Ceres. As the kernel "dies" in the soil only to be reborn as a plant, wheat—and the bread from which it is made—is also a durable icon of rebirth and thus immortality. Deities who "arose" from the dead and use ears of wheat as an emblem include Osiris (Egyptian), Tammuz (Babylonian), and Jesus (Christian). (See *Fruit*.)

OPPOSITE
"Bread or Revolution," the stark choice offered by the Industrial Workers of the World (IWW) in 1914. Although this unemployed worker is shown demonstrating in New York, social unrest tied to hunger was a global issue: a bread riot in Petrograd, Russia contributed to the forced abdication of Tsar Nicholas II in 1917.

2
Anpanman, an iconoclastic superhero created by Japanese artist Takashi Yanase in 1973. *Anpan* is a bread filled with sweet red bean paste that serves as Anpanman's edible head, which he offers to hungry children. Anpanman may appear Western, but his essence —symbolized by the red bean paste—is thoroughly Japanese.

3
Eight golden ears of wheat
emanate from a central, floriated
motif like rays of light, infusing
this bread plate—as well as the
bread on which it is served—with
solar and rebirth symbolism. Designed by British architect A.W.N.
Pugin in the Gothic Revival
style. England, earthenware with
colored glazes, c. 1850.

4

enriched bread, a 1965 screen print by American artist Corita Kent. The milled composite of individual wheat kernels, bread represents both nourishment and unity. Kent extends this symbolism with a quote from Albert Camus, who writes that hope is "nourished" by the daily deeds of "millions of solitary individuals."

5

Likely intended for the revels associated with peasant weddings in the Renaissance, this bawdy gingerbread mold features a nude, aroused couple. Eating bread baked from this mold would allow one to figuratively ingest the sexual power of its lovers. Austria, earthenware with lead glaze, c. 1475–1500.

6

An earthenware bread stamp from Egypt, 700–1300. The Arabic inscription in Kufic script reads *kull hani'an,* "Eat healthily!" Flat breads were commonly stamped throughout the ancient Levant to identify bakers and mark consecrated loaves with religious symbols. This exhortation to eat well is more surprising.

7

Having attained suffrage only the year before, German women— *Frauen!*—are pointedly addressed in this 1919 election poster by Lucian Bernhard. The message implores women to vote "for peace and bread!" This was the first national election to follow Germany's surrender in WWI.

The book is both secular and ecclesiastic: it represents the accumulated wisdom derived through scholarship as well as the divine truths acquired through revelation. It can signify a canon of accepted thought, the rule of law, or the word of gods in text-centric religions such as Christianity, Islam, or Judaism. With few exceptions the form of the book is a mark of authority. In Japanese, the *kanji* character for "book" is "origin" (*hon*).

As an emblem of learning and unfettered access to knowledge, the book is by extension a symbol of freedom. Liberty, liberal, library—all are derived from the Latin *liber,* meaning both "free" and "book." John Milton's 1644 polemic against censorship, *Areopagitica,* equates the book with human life itself, declaring "For Books are not absolutely dead things, but doe contain a potencie of life in them to be as active as that soule was whose progeny they are." In Chinese tradition the "leaves of the book are the leaves of the Cosmic Tree, symbolizing all beings in the universe" [Cooper]. The book is thus the cosmos, with each of its pages representing a human life. (See *Tree.*)

The physicality of the book, its "object-ness," is fundamental to its meaning: its heft, design, age, and smell all contribute to our reading and sensory experiences. Although Russian artist El Lissitsky called for the dematerialization of the book in 1926, the advent of the screen-based "e-book" is a relatively recent development. The separation of the book's traditional form from its contents is engendering a shift in the book's traditional meanings. It appears that a "disembodied" book is both more than, and less than, a book.

1

1
Open books merge with the sky to suggest freedom and limitless potential in this celebratory poster for "Book Day" sponsored by Barcelona's Official Book Chamber. The detail of the bird in flight reinforces the aspirational symbolism. Designed by Spanish artist Josep Morell Macías, c. 1930.

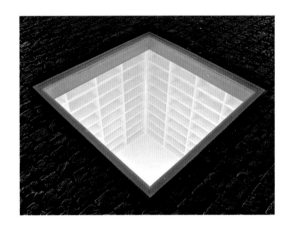

2
An ex libris of Amenhotep III and Queen Tiye of Egypt, c. 1391–1354 BCE. The hieroglyphic inscription reads, in part, "the book of the moringa tree." The expense and durability of this faience book-plate is significant: establishing the ownership of the royal library is as important as identifying its contents.

3
Books signify the flowering of thought and literary culture in this publisher's signet for Gerhard Stalling by German designer O.H.W. Hadank (c. 1921). A closed book signifies secret or unattainable knowledge; by contrast, the open books in this signet are invitational. The text reads, "The flower garden."

4
Inspired by the university's motto *Fiat Lux,* or "Let There Be Light," the trademark for the University of California Press in Berkeley depicts an open book with the recto (right-hand) page as a window. This book thus illuminates, in both senses of the word. Trademark by American graphic designer Mark Fox, 2005.

5
In a 1933 ritual of "purification" the Nazis burned approximately 20,000 books they deemed "un-German" at Opernplatz in Berlin. A 1995 memorial designed by Israeli sculptor Micha Ullman marks the event. Sunk into the plaza are bookshelves emptied of their books, a metaphoric tomb for the loss of culture.

DEUTSCHE LUFTHANSA

AIRPLANE

Derived from the Late Greek *aeroplanos,* the word "airplane" literally means "wandering in the air." To levitate or fly is to liberate oneself from physical constraints; to metaphorically access the spiritual. Associated with transcendence, the bird was mankind's original model for flight, and Italian inventor and artist Leonardo da Vinci based the design of his 15th-century ornithopter on the principle of flapping wings. (See *Bird.*)

The bird's-eye view offered the first aeronauts a power formerly reserved for omniscient sky gods. That power was quickly assumed by governments and put to use as early as the Napoleanic Wars (using hot air balloons). Although aerial reconnaissance is now largely conducted by satellites and unmanned drones equipped with live video feed, the airplane continues to enable superhuman vision. (See *Eye.*)

Speed and technological currency are crucial aspects of the airplane's symbolism. Aerodynamic forms helped define modernism in the 1920s and '30s, and were integral to streamlined architecture and design. Coinciding with the "jet age" of the mid-1950s, the American automotive industry affixed airplane hood ornaments to their cars in a similar bid for modernity.

Airplanes remain potent symbols of fear and the horrors of warfare: Guernica, Pearl Harbor, Dresden, Hiroshima, Operation Rolling Thunder, the Twin Towers. As one's point of view of an attacking aircraft is typically from the ground, the airplane's silhouette has become a powerful and recurring visual motif over the last 100 years.

OPPOSITE
German designer Ludwig Hohlwein's 1936 poster for Deutsche Lufthansa creates a visual link between commercial aviation and mythic flight. Coinciding with the Berlin Olympics, Hohlwein's heroic figure would seem to be a male counterpart to winged Nike, Greek goddess of victory.

2
Birdman: German civil engineer and inventor Otto Lilienthal in his "Sailing Apparatus," c. 1895. Lilienthal's aviation experiments preceded the work of the Wright Brothers in America, and contributed to their development of the first successful engine-powered aircraft in 1903.

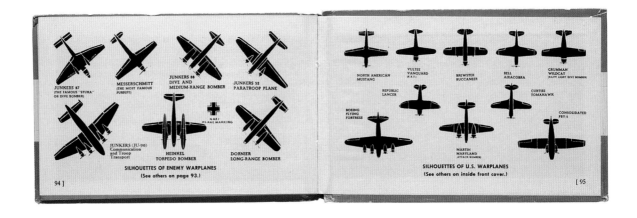

3

"To the advancement of motor transportation." This 1933 medallion, issued to commemorate the twenty-fifth anniversary of General Motors, is by American designer Norman Bel Geddes. Adding wings to a streamlined body transforms the earth-bound vehicle into something more mythic: an airplane.

4

Post-revolution, the emerging Soviet state understood that its survival depended on modernization. Airplanes—like trains, trams, and generators—functioned as shorthand symbols of this national aspiration. Red Aviator cookies packaging by Russian Constructivist Aleksandr Rodchenko, 1923.

5

Silhouettes of enemy and domestic warplanes are printed on the last page and inside back cover of *A Handbook of Civilian Defense*, published in the United States in 1942. The romance of aviation has given way to the airplane as a symbol of foreign aggression that incites fear.

7

8

6
Contemporary Chinese paper money issued by the Bank of the Dead and intended as a burnt offering. The airplane on this banknote can be seen as a mythic—but modern—messenger, able to quickly ferry money to the deceased for their use in the afterlife.

7
A US Navy F/A-18 Super Hornet approaching the speed of sound and creating a signature water vapor cone. The airplane has always served as a marker of technological and scientific achievement. Not only does this plane defy gravity, it defies human conceptions of speed that have existed for millennia.

8
New fears #5, a 2001 pastel drawing by American artist Chandra Cerrito. The September 11 terrorist attacks against the Twin Towers transformed the commercial airline into a weapon of religious warfare. The boundaries between military and civilian aircraft are now blurred.

CROSS
CIRCLE
CONCENTRIC CIRCLES
SQUARE
TRIANGLE
LOZENGE
SPIRAL
TRISKELE
SWASTIKA

abstract

CROSS

The superimposition of two strokes, one vertical and one horizontal, creates an equilateral cross with a central, common point. It is at this nexus that the vertical heaven meets the horizontal earth; where the creator meets the created; where male meets female. (The latter meaning prompted Viennese architect Adolf Loos to declare the cross an "erotic" ornament in 1910.) The union of opposites inherent in the cross' form thus makes it a symbol of harmony, balance, and completion. (See *Triangle.*)

As a mathematical "plus" sign, the cross conveys addition or union. The mathematical sign for division—the obelus—can be seen as a cross in which the two strokes fail to achieve union. The unbroken horizontal stroke is fully realized; the vertical stroke is cleaved in two.

With its four arms of equal length, the cross shares in the symbolism of the number four. In pre-Columbian Mesoamerica the cross was a sun sign associated with the four cardinal points and the four winds. As the winds bring life-giving rain, the equilateral cross also functioned as an emblem of fertility.

The cross inscribed in a circle—a sun cross—can represent the center of a sacred space. Among Neolithic German tribes, the sun cross denoted the sun or fire. Breaking the sun cross at four points along its periphery forms a circular swastika; to the idea of the cross as center is added rotational dynamism: the cross as vortex. (See *Sun; Swastika.*)

In Africa, the cross can symbolize the crossroads, a place of transition and danger where the paths of the living cross with the paths of the dead.

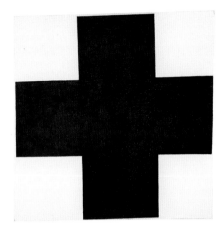

1
Russian artist Kazimir Malevich painted a series of "new icons" between 1915 and 1923, among them the *Black Cross* (1915). Malevich's cross is both funerary and celebratory: it signals the death of representational art as it announces the birth of Suprematism.

2
What appears to be a sun cross is actually a reductive Japanese depiction of a horse's bit. Known as *Kutsuwa,* the design was used as a family crest (*mon*) by the powerful Shimazu clan in the late 16th and early 17th centuries.

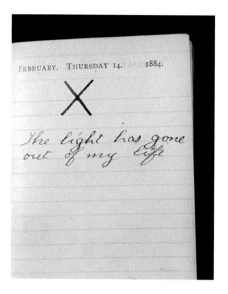

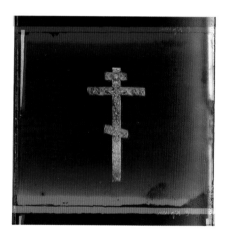

3

A central cross is flanked by four swastikas, each of which is demarcated by four yellow Tau crosses. Both the swastika and the Tau cross are Viking representations of Thor's hammer, a symbol of the thunderbolt, rain, fertility, and good luck. From the Oseberg burial mound, Norway, brass and cloisonné, c. 850.

4

Rotated forty-five degrees the equilateral cross becomes an X, a mark associated with opposition or cancellation (i.e. to "cross out"). Upon the deaths of his wife and mother on the same day in 1884, US President Theodore Roosevelt made the following diary entry: "The light has gone out of my life."

5

This Hopi cross denotes an unmarried girl. Its form is representational: the short arms of the cross are based on the distinctive hair whorls worn by young Hopi women until the first half of the 20th century.

6

The word "cross" stems from the Latin verb *cruciare*, meaning "to torture." Originally a symbol of shame, the Roman cross of public execution ultimately became *the* icon of Christianity. The trichrome photograph of this Russian crucifix was taken by Sergei Mikhailovich Prokudin-Gorskii in 1911.

7

The Biete Ghiorgis, or House of St. George, a 13th-century Ethiopian Orthodox church in Lalibela, Ethiopia. Carved from solid rock in a cruciform silhouette, to enter the church is to enter the cross, "a point of communication between heaven and earth" [Cooper].

8

The House of Terror (*Terror Háza*) is a museum in Budapest, Hungary, dedicated to examining the crimes of the WWII-era fascist Arrow Cross Party. The emblem of the Arrow Cross—visible at the roofline—is an aggressive symbol of continuous outward expansion. External facade by architect Attila F. Kovács, 2002.

9

If splayed to simultaneously reveal its front and back, the design on this poncho forms a short-armed cross. To wear this textile is to become literally and symbolically *central*: the arms of four concentric crosses—red, black, ochre, and green—emanate from the head like a woven nimbus. Peru, Andes, 400–800 CE.

CIRCLE

Seemingly without beginning or end, the circle's silhouette is continuous and omnidirectional, and so serves as a symbol of eternity, timelessness, and immortality. Its form is associated with the sun and moon; solar and lunar cycles (and thus rebirth); the "dome" of the heavens; and the eye of sun gods. It represents unity and totality—as in the circular *yin* and *yang*—as well as wholeness (and, linguistically, holiness.) Whereas the square is static and earthly, the circle is dynamic and celestial. (See *Sun; Moon; Square.*)

The circle may be used to create a protective boundary or demarcate sacred space. The Egyptian hieroglyph *shen,* whose name is derived from the verb "to encircle," is the basis of the cartouche, the ovoid glyph that encloses written royal names. Like the *shen* ring, the cartouche "took on the connotation of protection—as the device which excluded all inimical elements from the royal name" [Wilkinson]. The belief in the apotropaic power of the circle extends to jewelry that encircles the body: the ring, bracelet, arm band, necklace, and crown.

To draw a circle with a compass one must first determine the center point. The word "center"— Latin *centrum,* Greek *kentron*—is derived from the verb "to prick," which describes the action of the compass' spike on a substrate. Whether articulated or merely implied the center is crucial to both the circle's form and meaning. To be at the circle's center is to be balanced and in harmony; to be outside the center is to be unbalanced and *eccentric.* (See *Concentric Circles.*)

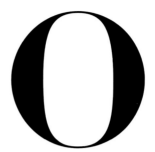

OPPOSITE
Three circles in three shades of blue form a ritual diagram intended to sharpen the senses and memory of religious acolytes. In Tantric tradition the circular form may reference a *shaligram,* an aniconic stone symbol of the Hindu god Vishnu. Near Sanganer, India, pigment on paper, 2005.

2
As a placeholder in mathematics, the form of the zero—ovoid and egg-like—suggests numeric potential. Rather than signifying emptiness or nothing, the zero can be understood as "a pregnant void" [Ronnberg and Martin]. A numeral zero in the typeface Didot B64 Bold by American type designer Jonathan Hoefler, 1991.

3

Set within an older, Neolithic earthen ring, the circle of stones known as Stonehenge is Britain's largest Bronze Age cremation cemetery. While its uses have varied over time, as a burial site Stonehenge's circular ground plan likely held protective significance for both the living and the dead. And, like the mandala design of a Hindu temple, it may be considered a symbolic map of the world, a cosmos in miniature with a central, sacred point. By American photographer Marilyn Bridges, 1985. Wiltshire, England, c. 2600–1600 BCE. DETAIL

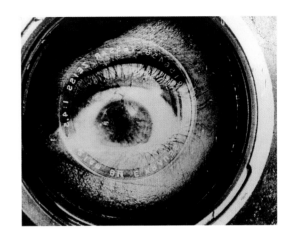

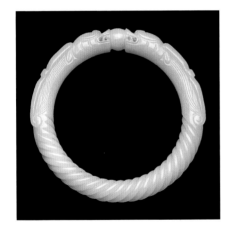

4

Mercury, the god of commerce and communications, appears on this poster stamp for the Vienna International Trade Fair. The pattern of circles is an artifact of the punched paper tape used by telex machines at that time and signals the speed of modern messaging. By Austrian designer Wilhelm Jaruska, 1970.

5

A still from Soviet director Dziga Vertov's self-reflexive documentary film *Man with a Movie Camera*, 1929. A montage of two circular apertures—camera lens and eye—suggests an impartial, mechanized vision. In this context, the circle is linked with perception and focus, and perhaps even truth.

6

Two facing dragons form a closed loop on this Qing dynasty jade bracelet. The auspicious meanings are many: the circle suggests harmony and protection; the dragons embody a felicitous meeting or reunion. The circle is completed by a second, smaller circle: the dragons' shared pearl. China, c. 1700–1800.

7

Five interlocking rings—symbol of Olympic unity—become loops of barbed wire that limit civilian dissent in this 1968 poster by the Atelier Populaire Marseille in France. Days before the start of the Mexico City Olympic Games, the government quashed student protesters in what became known as the Tlatelolco massacre.

CONCENTRIC CIRCLES

In its simplest form—a dot within a circle—concentric circles represent *essence* or *point of origin:* the germ at the core of a seed, the child within its mother's womb, or the body's soul. In all three examples, the outer circle functions as a physical perimeter. The dot and circle can also depict the sun and its corona, which, by extension, symbolizes light, the solar metal gold, and "the open eye of God" [Koch]. In these instances, the outermost circle is an emanation. (See *Sun; Eye.*)

Two open, concentric circles form the Egyptian hieroglyph for "sun" or "day." To the Chumash Indians of the California coast, three concentric circles form a shamanistic portal, a symbol of moving from one world or state of consciousness to another. The three circles' common center may be regarded as an *omphalos* (or navel), a sacred point of contact between the terrestrial and the celestial. Rather than emanating out, however, the visual flow is inward, toward the center.

Conceived as a three-dimensional mandala, the 9th-century Buddhist temple at Borobudur, Java, is surmounted by three concentric circular terraces that lead to a central stupa. As one ascends the terraces toward the stupa, the journey becomes a symbol of "the progressive concentric movement towards the discovery of the self" [Chevalier and Gheerbrant].

In the context of a map, concentric circles typically signify the locus of an urban center. Whether marking the epicenter of a disaster or diagraming Dante's nine circles of Hell, the innermost ring identifies a phenomenon's most potent point.

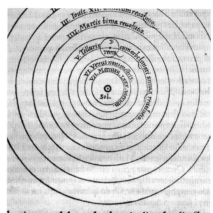

1

2

1

Nicolaus Copernicus' heliocentric diagram from *De revolutionibus orbium coelestium,* or *On the Revolutions of the Heavenly Spheres,* published in 1543. Concentric circles mark planetary orbits in this notable challenge to Ptolemy's geocentric model of the cosmos. DETAIL

2

Concentric circles with alternating light and dark halves create a stylized *t'aeguk,* a symbol of the "unity of opposites," more commonly known as *yin* and *yang.* This 10 mun postage stamp was issued by the Joseon Dynasty, Korea, in 1884.

3
Muslim pilgrims at prayer form
a series of radiating rings around
the Ka'aba, the cube-like structure in Mecca, Saudi Arabia, that
houses the Black Stone. Pilgrims
circumambulate the Ka'aba like
planets orbiting the sun, symbolically fixing the axis of the world in
the center of the Grand Mosque.

4
The Akan people of present-day
Ghana understand three or four
concentric circles as *adinkrahene* or adinkra king: chief of all
Adinkra symbols. Stamped on
cloth in combination with other
designs, the *adinkrahene* signifies
greatness or leadership.

5
The blue double circle in this
Japanese sake cup is known
as *Jya no me* or snake eye. Its
presence is practical: if the color
of the sake between the outer
and inner circle is slightly yellow,
it indicates that the sake was
improperly stored. (Good-quality
filtered sake should be clear.)
Interestingly, Japanese school-
teachers mark correct exam
answers with a circle and superior
answers with a double circle.
In this context, two concentric
circles signal importance or
excellence.

SQUARE

Symmetrical, equilateral, void of curves and diagonals, the square epitomizes stability, immutability, and thus permanence. Unlike the circle, which is infinite and dynamic, the square is finite and fixed: of man-made forms, it is the irreducible unit, the essence, the *punkt*.

In contrast to the "dome" of the heavens, the square is the earth and the material plane. One can posit that the circle signifies the *creator* while the square denotes the *created*—an idea elegantly expressed in sacred architecture by the domed temple rising from its square foundation. The square also represents order and rational creation, and public squares are a common feature of urban centers in medieval Europe.

When three-dimensional, the square and its association with static perfection is amplified. Religious texts or relics that are intrinsically resistant to change are appropriately stored in cubic structures: Jewish tefillin are black leather quadrate boxes that contain passages from the Torah; Islam's *Ka'aba* (or Cube) houses the Black Stone, an object of Muslim veneration.

Early in the 20th century avant-garde artists adopted the square as a signifier of the "new." The inert, "zero" form of the 1915 painting *Black Square* allowed Russian artist Kazimir Malevich to symbolically kill representational art while simultaneously introducing non-objective Suprematism. With his book *About Two Squares* (1922), El Lissitzky links the square to the creation of the new Soviet state, imploring his readers to "build."

OPPOSITE
German designer Fritz Schleifer uses the square as an elemental building block for both type and image in this 1923 exhibition poster. One red square—the eye—signals the new vision of the Weimar Bauhaus (or Build House).

2
Comprised of two cubes, the Namaz Khaneh is a Muslim prayer room in Tehran, Iran. As an aid to prayer and contemplation, the inner cube is aligned to Mecca and both cubes are open to the sky. Designed by Iranian architect Kamran Diba in 1978. (The architectural model is shown.)

3

The Great Chrysanthemum
Necklace from the 2007 Stolen
Jewels collection by American
industrial design studio Mike
& Maaike. The squares that
comprise the necklace—leather
"pixels"—are derived from an enlarged lo-res image "stolen" from
the internet. While the square
has traditionally signified

resistance to change, the pixel
presents a paradoxical twist. Even
as the form of the square pixel
remains constant, it nonetheless
facilitates the endless mutation
of digital imagery—and thus of
impermanence.

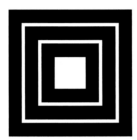

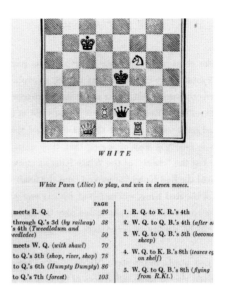

WHITE

White Pawn (Alice) to play, and win in eleven moves.

	PAGE		
meets R. Q.	26	I.	R. Q. to K. R.'s 4th
through Q.'s 3d (by railway)	38	2.	W. Q. to Q. B.'s 4th (after sl
's 4th (Tweedledum and eedledee)	50	3.	W. Q. to Q. B.'s 5th (become sheep)
meets W. Q. (with shawl)	70	4.	W. Q. to K. B.'s 8th (leaves eg on shelf)
to Q.'s 5th (shop, river, shop)	78		
to Q.'s 6th (Humpty Dumpty)	86	5.	W. Q. to Q. B.'s 8th (flying from R.Kt.)
to Q.'s 7th (forest)	103		

4

The Japanese *masu* is a square wooden box used for measuring rice in the 8th century, when rice was a form of currency. *Masu* is a homophone with the word for "increase," and these three concentric squares—three *masu*—can be understood as a symbol of abundance. This *mon* serves as the crest of the Ichikawa clan.

5

Originating in India, chess' sixty-four squares recreate the cosmos and its innumerable choices. The alternating squares are dualistic: light and dark, male and female, etc. Lewis Carroll's table of contents for *Through the Looking-Glass* (1871) uses the chessboard as a temporal and spatial map of Alice's world. DETAIL

6

To the ancient Chinese the square symbolized the earth and the circle represented the heavens. The terrestrial and celestial are figuratively united on this Imperial *cash* coin (c. 1850), creating a balance and harmony that expresses the ideals of *yin* and *yang*.

7

Josef Albers' 1963 oil painting *Homage to the Square: Aglow*. Over several decades the artist explored the relative nature of color perception within the tight parameters of nested squares. Albers' square functions as a scientific control: it is a neutral constant among a range of variables.

1435 Vue de la pyramide de Chéops pendant

TRIANGLE

The triangle frequently represents triadic concepts, among them: world (air, water, land); time (past, present, future); family (man, woman, child); and lifespan (birth, life, death). *Two* is often oppositional and binary; in contrast, *three* offers a creative alternative to dualism. The triangle thus becomes a symbol of synthesis, wholeness, or all.

Apex up, the equilateral triangle signifies the sun, the sun god, fire, and heat. It is also a fertility symbol: like the three-lobed trefoil, the equilateral triangle represents the erect phallus. Inverted, apex down, the triangle suggests the heart; water or rain; the moon and its three phases; the goddess as genetrix; and the female mons pubis—what Vladimir Nabokov refers to as "the indigo delta" in his 1955 novel *Lolita*. (The ancient Sumerian glyph for "woman" is an inverted triangle with an articulated vulva.) Regardless of its orientation, the equilateral triangle is a symbol of life and of life force. (See *Sun; Fire; Heart*.)

Two triangles with their points touching, apex to apex, represent coitus. The resulting X-form is the procreative point of contact between the sexes, "the bindu, or 'seed' of manifestation" [Chevalier and Gheerbrant]. (See *Cross*.)

When two equilateral triangles are superimposed—one apex up, the other down—a hexagram is formed. This six-pointed star is a union of opposites: heaven and earth, sun and moon, male and female, fire and water. Like the equilateral cross or *yin* and *yang* it represents harmony, balance, and completion. (See *Star*.)

OPPOSITE
The Great Pyramid at Giza in Egypt, c. 2500 BCE. Originally faced with white limestone to reflect light, the pyramid is a monumental expression of sun and life symbolism that contrasts with its use as a mausoleum. Photograph by the French studio Maison Bonfils, before 1899.

2
An American fallout shelter sign issued by the Office of Civil Defense, c. 1961. While the intention may have been to identify a safe meeting point—three triangles "point" to the center—the sign has come to symbolize the Cold War and the threat of nuclear annihilation.

3

Two interlaced, equilateral triangles form a liquid, rotating hexagram on the interior of this 12th-century high-tin bronze bowl from Afghanistan. The six-pointed star is a reconciliation of duality that embodies harmony and balance. To Hindus, it expresses the sacred marriage of Shiva and Shakti; in alchemy, it merges the male fire with the female water; among Semitic peoples, it is known as the talismanic Seal of Solomon. As an emblem of synthesis and wholeness, the hexagram can be understood as an aniconic representation of divinity, "the logical symbol of heaven and of God" [Whittick].

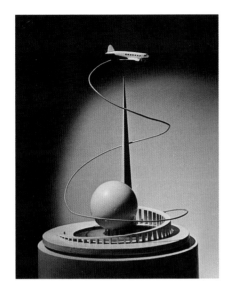

4

5

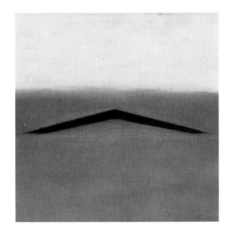

6

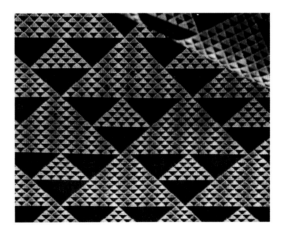

7

4
The New York World's Fair of 1939 advertised "The World of Tomorrow," and its most iconic structures were the Trylon and Perisphere. With a nod to the Bauhaus, the triangular pylon and sphere promised a modernist, utopian future to Depression-weary Americans. Model by Harrison & Foilhoux, architects.

5
Two triangles, placed apex to apex to form an X silhouette, can represent sexual union. A variation of this motif—the *copulatio*—is commonly incorporated into 18th- and 19th-century woven Anatolian kilim. The *copulatio* is "to be understood as a (feminine) X-shape perforated by a (masculine) rod" [Barbatti].

6
When seen from above, Maya Lin's design of the Vietnam Veterans Memorial is triangular, with the names of the war's first and last American casualties meeting at the apex. This effectively creates a closed (triangular) loop that serves to symbolize completion and thus resolution. Competition drawing, c. 1980.

7
This repeating pattern of triangles is known in Japan as *urokomon*, or fish-scale pattern. Derived from the skin of fish, the armor-like pattern was believed to repel evil spirits. Kimono and obi imprinted with the apotropaic motif were worn by women when they "became thirty-three, the 'unlucky year' (*yakudoshi*)" [Brown].

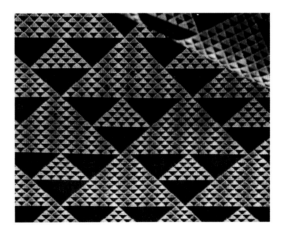

LOZENGE

Comprising two triangles, the lozenge (or diamond) is intimately connected to concepts of female fertility. It can represent the vulva as gateway, the womb as protected enclosure, or—when seen as a reductive silhouette—the female torso. It can and does represent all of these concepts simultaneously; just as the Latin word *mater* (mother) is linguistically tied to *matrix* (womb), so too the lozenge proposes a visual equivalence between mother and vulva. (See *Triangle.*)

Among the Berber weavers of Morocco the lozenge is the basic unit of a range of coded sexual signifiers. Depending on the context the diamond can communicate readiness for conception, pregnancy, or birth. Even the Berber eight-pointed star—with an implicit or explicit lozenge at its center—is a fertility symbol, with some Moroccans calling it "*moussrîoûla… which means her with the little knickers*" [Barbatti]. (See *Star.*)

The Wixárika (or Huichol) of Mexico also use the lozenge as the modular basis for many of their woven patterns. The diamond motif functions as a central, womb-like structure to elicit animating principles such as *water, life,* or *genesis,* especially in depictions of flora and fauna. For example, the interior of the double water-gourd may be demarcated with a lozenge; the ovule of the white tōtoˊ flower—linked with rain as it grows in the wet season—may be indicated by concentric lozenges. (See *Concentric Circles.*)

Connecting the lozenge's four points horizontally and vertically creates a cruciform design that is called "god's eye" by the Wixárika and "the eye of fire" by early Germanic tribes. The lozenge's center, whether as the pupil of an eye or as a child in utero, is fundamental to the symbol's meanings. (See *Cross; Eye.*)

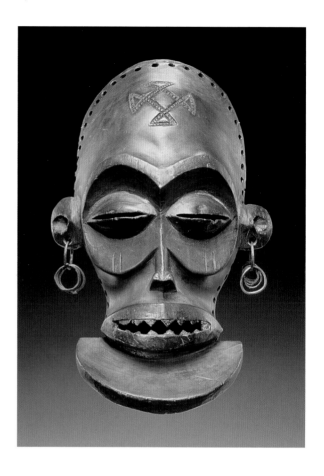

1
The forehead of this Cihongo mask is incised with the *cingely-engelye,* a design likely based on the Maltese cross. The endlessly looping motif with a lozenge at its core suggests eternity—and may symbolize the creator deity Nzambi. Chokwe, Democratic Republic of the Congo, carved wood.

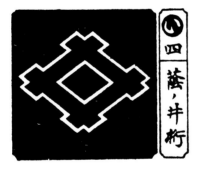

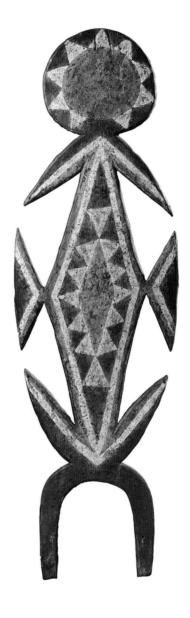

2

The Queene of Diamonds from a deck of English playing cards. While the gemstone is compared to "True Vertues" fit for a queen, as a reductive glyph the diamond is a life symbol equated with female sexuality. Its red coloration evokes vigor, passion, and blood. Block and stencil printing, 1720.

3

Worn at the Pig Feast to honor ancestors and ensure the continued fertility of pig herds, this dance headdress is known as *wenena gerua*. The anthropomorphic design combines male and female elements: the circular head is *for numuna*, or house of the sun; the diamond torso is *afaniki*, or hand of the moon. The torso's central, yellow diamond optically pulsates: surrounding red triangles lead the eye inward while alternating white triangles emanate out. *In* then *out*, the diamond breathes with life. Siane peoples, New Guinea, carved and painted wood, 20th century.

4

The Japanese family crest, *igeta*, depicts a wooden frame built across the mouth of a well. Although some *igeta* conform to a square, most versions feature a central lozenge. Water is *yin* and so associated with the female sex—the diamond-like representation may be an intentional nod to this linkage.

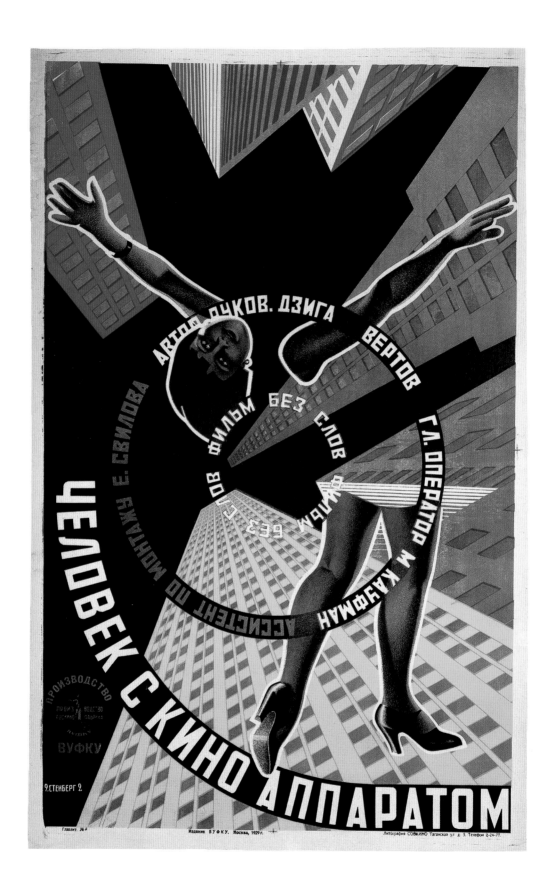

SPIRAL

The spiral is inherently dynamic and can represent natural phenomena such as the whirlwind, rolling thunder, or roiling waters. Its helical form mimics the natural growth patterns of mollusk shells and can signify exponential increase. (See *Snail.*)

The form of the spiral suggests potentiality: a latent power yet to be released, or a life yet to be lived. Unlike the immutable square, or concentric circles that emanate from a point of origin (and thus suggest the past), the unspooling spiral indicates the future. German photographer Karl Blossfeldt's 1928 photographs of young Maidenhair-Fern fronds exemplify this potential. (See *Square; Concentric Circles.*)

The S-shaped double spiral is a nearly universal form that evokes cyclical processes: the inhalation and exhalation of breath, the ebb and flow of tides, the waxing and waning of the moon, the rising and setting of the sun. It is departure and return, unwinding and winding, death and rebirth. Symmetrical and balanced, it is the Occidental equivalent of the Oriental *yin* and *yang.*

In European, Eurasian, and North African Neolithic symbolism the double spiral is believed to represent an umbilicus, "the link between foetus and matrix" [Barbatti], child and mother. It is a glyph intimately tied to concepts of female fertility, nourishment, growth, and emerging life. To the Hopi, Zuni, and other Pueblo peoples of the American Southwest, the double spiral is a symbolic map of their tribal migrations. Variations of a double-spiral petroglyph are found at Chaco Canyon, New Mexico, and at Mesa Verde, Colorado. (See *Swastika.*)

OPPOSITE
The spiraling design of this poster's typography suggests a film reel; as it unspools, the viewer is transported to another temporal and spatial reality. Russian poster artists Vladimir and Georgii Stenberg created this image of a cinematic vortex for Dziga Vertov's 1929 film *Man with a Movie Camera.*

2
An 1825 self-portrait of Maori warrior Te Pehi Kupe. The looping *koru* motifs on his cheeks derive from the unfurling fronds of the silver fern, a plant native to New Zealand. One *koru* suggests growth and life; two whorls, joined to form a shallow U, represent the head of the hammerhead shark and are a sign of power.

3
A circular staircase corkscrews
around an open core, creating a vertiginous effect. The
rotating spiral is used in cinema,
in particular, as a visual cue for
dream states or altered states of
consciousness. Ponce de Leon
Inlet lighthouse, Florida, 1887.

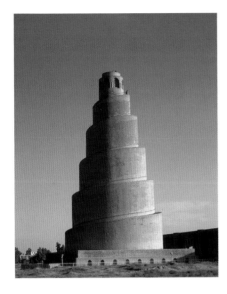

4

The 9th-century spiral minaret of the Great Mosque in Samarra, Iraq. As in the labyrinth at Chartres Cathedral, anyone climbing the minaret's stairs will ultimately be lead to the center—but at a height of 52 meters (170 feet). In this context, physical ascension is analogous to spiritual ascension and thus enlightenment.

5

The pavement labyrinth in Chartres Cathedral, France, c. 1200. While not a spiral in the simplest sense, this unicursal maze nonetheless requires pilgrims walking its path to conduct a series of loops to reach the center. To medieval Christians this circuitous path may have symbolized the arduous pilgrimage to Jerusalem.

6

Four interconnected whorls—creating four pairs of double spirals—evoke the cyclic path of the sun on this Iron Age "picture stone." Painted on a memorial to the dead, the rotating solar motif likely represents a cycle of life, death, and rebirth. Gotland, Sweden, 5th century. DETAIL

7

"Photo 51," an X-ray diffraction image of DNA taken by British molecular biologists Rosalind Franklin and Raymond Gosling in 1952. This image proved pivotal to the understanding and mapping of DNA's molecular structure. Its double helix—two spirals winding around each other—symbolizes life on a genetic level.

TRISKELE

The *triskele*—literally, three-legged—is an Aegean design with kinetic dynamism, each of its curved or bent legs operating like a fan blade to optically propel the form. Like the swastika, the triskele is a symbol of power, ceaseless energy, and by extension, immortality. Unlike the typical swastika, however, the triskele's legs are often alive: literal human limbs with thighs, calves, and feet; or comprised of winged animals or the heads of beasts. (See *Swastika.*)

The triskele is thought to be solar or lunar in origin, in which case the legs may serve as markers of time or celestial position to indicate the sun's "rising, zenith and setting" [Cooper], or the moon's three phases. As a solar sign the triskele would additionally signify light, life, cyclical regeneration, and rebirth. In antiquity it was considered an auspicious symbol. (See *Sun.*)

Roman versions sometimes place the head of Medusa at the triskele's central axis, thereby magnifying the symbol's apotropaic powers. (Including the severed head of Medusa implies the protection of the goddess Athena.) The triskele, with or without Medusa, has symbolized the triangular island of Sicily since at least the 1st century BCE.

Since the 20th century the triskele has been adopted by various fascist and neo-fascist movements to represent their "revolutionary" beliefs, among them the South African white separatist *Afrikaner Weerstandsbeweging* (or Afrikaner Resistance Movement). Breton separatists have used a triple spiral, which combines the power symbolism of the triskele with the spiral's evocation of growth. (See *Spiral.*)

1

1
Three interlaced birds identify the Ravenswood Winery in this poster by American designer David Lance Goines (1979). Like the Korean tricolor *t'aeguk,* Goines' ravens rotate *in,* toward the central axis in a display of centripetal force. This animate triskele exemplifies the concept of unity or common purpose.

2

A 25 pfennig banknote designed by Jos. Dominicus in 1920 for the German city of Paderborn. The *notgeld* (or emergency money) features the Paderborn Cathedral's window of three hares (16th century). Thought to represent the Christian concept of Trinity, the three hares become "one" via their shared ears.

3

Coins minted under the Lycian dynast Mithrapata tend to include a small triskele with his image; this example uses a portrait-sized triskele with his name instead. Here the triskele likely represents Mithrapata and, as he is named for the Persian god of light, it may symbolize Mithra as well. 380–370 BCE.

4

A trademark for Atlantic Refining by American designer Seymour Robins, c. 1965. A triangular letter *A* forms the basis of this monogram-as-triskele. Intended primarily for use on service station signs, the spinning emblem evokes the torquing force of the gasoline engine.

SWASTIKA

An equilateral cross with "bent" arms, the swastika combines the cross' symbolism of *union* and *center* with rotational dynamism. The result is an animate cross: a whirling junction of heaven and earth, male and female, that suggests creative and procreative life force. Historically an emblem of blessing and good fortune, its Sanskrit name *Svastika* assures us "It is well." (See *Cross*.)

As a solar sign the swastika may have evolved from the sun cross or four-spoked sun wheel. Like its three-legged cousin the triskele, the swastika can signify the sun, cyclical renewal, rebirth, and immortality. It is an attribute of sky, sun, and fire gods, among them Dyaus (Indo-Aryan), Indra and Agni (Indian), Zeus and Helios (Greek), Jupiter (Roman), and Thor (Norse). It is also associated with the heart of Buddha and, to some early Christians, the promised return of the Messiah. (See *Sun; Wheel; Triskele*.)

To the Hopi the swastika is a record of their tribal migrations that maps a cycle of departure and return. The center of the swastika is *Tuwanasavi,* a world axis that corresponds to Hopi territory in the American southwest; each swastika arm represents one of four clan migrations that lead out from the swastika's center, only to return.

Adolf Hitler adopted the swastika as a symbol of national rebirth, but the Nazi concept of Germany's post-Weimar renewal entailed "purifying" the nation with mass incarcerations and killings. His appropriation of the auspicious *Hakenkreuz* (or hooked cross) as a racist symbol has resulted in its connotative contamination. The swastika now simultaneously signifies both good *and* evil: a life symbol that is equated with death and "can still… conjure a world of horror" [Heller].

OPPOSITE
Horses can be solar or lunar, depending on the context. In a procession beneath crowing cocks and flanked by floating swastikas, however, these horses appear to be part of a solar narrative in which the swastikas are sun signs. The Bernoulli Jug from the Greek island of Skyros, painted pottery, c. 580–560 BCE.

2
By the early 20th century the swastika was a universally popular symbol of felicity, appearing in corporate advertising and branding, on textiles, and as an architectural motif. The Fernie Swastikas—a Canadian female hockey team—are shown wearing the good luck symbol as their team insignia, c. 1922.

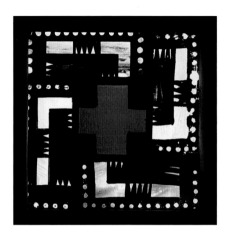

⊓⌐ ⊑⊤⌐⌐⌐

3

A gilded Buddhist swastika, or *manji*, marks the apex of the gabled roof at Senso-ji Temple in Tokyo. In both China and Japan the swastika is equated with the number 10,000 and symbolizes the idea of *all:* "the uncountable, that is to say all existence in the phenomenal world" [Cooper].

4

The relationship between the equilateral cross and the swastika is foregrounded in this stained glass window by French artist Marguerite Huré. The design emphasizes the swastika's hub, which, for Christians, is Christ: the intercessor between humanity and divinity. Notre-Dame du Raincy, France, 1923.

5

Dutch painter Theo van Doesburg's 1917 masthead for the periodical *De Stijl* (The Style). Based on the square and rectangle, a fragmented swastika serves as the masthead's letter *S*—and embodies the dynamic, revolutionary nature of De Stijl's non-representational approach.

6

"The People Vote List 1." Voters swarm to a monumental swastika from the four cardinal directions on this Nazi campaign poster from 1932. As if marking one of the earth's poles, the design implies that the nexus of the swastika—as well as of National Socialism—aligns with the center and heart of Germany.

BIBLIOGRAPHY
INDEX
IMAGE CREDITS
COLOPHON
ACKNOWLEDGMENTS

Armstrong, Helen, ed. *Graphic Design Theory: Readings from the Field*. New York: Princeton Architectural Press, 2009.

Ayto, John. *Bloomsbury Dictionary of Word Origins*. London: Bloomsbury, 1990.
  CITATION: Teeth, p. 536.

Barbatti, Bruno. *Berber Carpets of Morocco: The Symbols*. Paris: ACR Édition, 2008.
  CITATIONS: Triangle, as *copulatio*, p. 181; Lozenge, p. 21; Spiral, p. 27.

Bartholomew, Terese Tse. *Hidden Meanings in Chinese Art*. San Francisco: Asian Art Museum and Chong-Moon Lee Center for Asian Art and Culture, 2006.

Betsky, Aaron, ed. *Icons: Magnets of Meaning*. San Francisco: San Francisco Museum of Modern Art and Chronicle Books, 1997.

Biedermann, Hans. *Dictionary of Symbolism*. New York: Meridian, 1994.
  CITATION: Eye, as mouth, p. 123.

Borchardt-Hume, Achim, ed. *Albers and Moholy-Nagy: From the Bauhaus to the New World*. New Haven, CT: Yale University Press, 2006.

Brody, J.J. *Mimbres Painted Pottery*. Santa Fe: School of American Research Press, 2004.

Brown, Kendall H., ed. *Deco Japan: Shaping Art & Culture, 1920–1945*. Alexandria, VA: Art Services international, 2012.
  CITATION: Triangle, as *urokomon*, p. 193.

Cabarga, Leslie. *A Treasury of German Trademarks: Volume One, 1850–1925*. New York: Art Direction Book Company, 1982.

——. *A Treasury of German Trademarks, Volume Two, 1900–1950*. New York: Art Direction Book Company, 1985.

Chevalier, Jean, and Alain Gheerbrant. *Dictionary of Symbols*. London and New York: Penguin Books, 1996.
  CITATIONS: Lion, p. 613; Bird, p. 89; Seashell, p. 228; Serpent, p. 844; Concentric Circles, p. 201; Triangle: p. 1035.

Christianson, Scott. *100 Diagrams That Changed the World: From the Earliest Cave Painting to the Innovation of the iPod*. London: Plume, 2012.

Cooper, J.C. *An Illustrated Encyclopaedia of Traditional Symbols*. London: Thames and Hudson, 1978.
  CITATIONS: Tree, as Christmas tree, p. 177; Flower, p. 100; Cock, p. 38; Crow/Raven, with heron, p. 83; Fish, p. 68; Serpent, impaled by arrow, p. 15; Book, p. 24; Cross, as architecture, p. 45; Triskele, p. 181; Swastika, p. 170.

Dabrowski, Magdalena, Leah Dickerman, and Peter Galassi. *Aleksandr Rodchenko*. New York: The Museum of Modern Art, 1998.

Eagleton, Catherine, and Jonathan Williams. *Money: A History*. London: The British Museum Press, 2006.

Eidelberg, Martin, ed. *Design 1935–1965: What Modern Was*. New York: Musée des Arts Décoratifs de Montréal and Henry N. Abrams, 1991.

Ekhtiar, Maryam, and Priscilla Soucek, eds. *Masterpieces from the Department of Islamic Art in The Metropolitan Museum of Art*. New York: The Metropolitan Museum of Art, 2011.

Enciso, Jorge. *Design Motifs of Ancient Mexico*. New York: Dover Publications, 1953.

Fazzioli, Edoardo. *Chinese Calligraphy from Pictograph to Ideogram*. New York: Abbeville Press, 1987.

Fine Arts Museums of San Francisco. *Africa, Oceania, the Americas, and The Jolika Collection of New Guinea Art*. San Francisco: Fine Arts Museums of San Francisco, 2009.

Fontana, David. *The Secret Language of Symbols: A Visual Key to Symbols and Their Meanings*. San Francisco: Chronicle Books, 1994.
  CITATIONS: Octopus, p. 89; Twins, as Gemini sign, p. 165.

Frédéric, Louis. *Japan Encyclopedia*. Cambridge: Harvard University Press, 2002.
  CITATION: Dog, as *Inu hariko*, p. 391.

Geertz, Clifford. *Negara: The Theatre State in Nineteenth-Century Bali.* Princeton: Princeton University Press, 1980.
CITATION: Door/Gate, as passage through Mount Meru, p. 228.

Haeckel, Ernst. *Art Forms in Nature.* Munich and New York: Prestel, 1998.

Hawley, W. M., and Kei Kaneda Chappelear. *Mon: The Japanese Family Crest.* Self-published, 1976.

Heller, Steven. *Iron Fists: Branding the 20th-Century Totalitarian State.* London and New York: Phaidon Press, 2008.
CITATION: Swastika, p. 75.

——. *The Swastika: A Symbol Beyond Redemption?.* New York: Allworth Press, 2000.

—— and Karen Pomeroy. *Design Literacy: Understanding Graphic Design.* New York: Allworth Press, 1997.

Hornung, *Clarence P. Handbook of Designs and Devices.* New York: Dover Publications, 1959.
CITATION: Egg, p. 205.

Jaffé, Aniela. "Symbolism in the visual arts" in Carl Jung, *Man and His Symbols.* London: Aldus Books Limited, 1964.

Jamme, Franck André. *Tantra Song: Tantric Paintings from Rajasthan.* Los Angeles: Siglio, 2011.

Jereb, James F. *Arts & Crafts of Morocco.* San Francisco: Chronicle Books, 1996.

Kamekura, Yusaka and Paul Rand. *Trademark Designs of the World.* New York: Dover Publications, 1981.

Kinsey, Alfred Charles. *Sexual Behavior in the Human Female.* Bloomington: Indiana University Press, 1953.

Kjellgren, Eric. *How to Read Oceanic Art.* New York: The Metropolitan Museum of Modern Art, 2014.

Koch, Rudolf. *The Book of Signs.* New York: Dover Publications, 1955.
CITATIONS: Moon, as glyph, p. 93; Concentric Circles, p. 2.

Kurstin, Joseph. *Netsuke: Story Carvings of Old Japan.* Self-published, 1994.

—— and Gilles Lorin. *The Peacock's Feather: Gentlemen Jewelry of Old Japan.* Self-published, 2007.

LaGamma, Alisa, and Christine Giuntini. *The Essential Art of African Textiles: Design Without End.* New York: The Metropolitan Museum of Art, 2008.

Leal, Marcia Castro. *Archaeological Mexico.* Firenze: Casa Editrice Bonechi, 1990.

Levy, Dana, Lea Sneider, and Frank B. Gibney. *Kanban: the Art of the Japanese Shop Sign.* San Francisco: Chronicle Books, 1983.

Lilly, Simon. *Ancient Celtic Coin Art.* Glastonbury: Wooden Books, 2008.

Liungman, Carl. *Dictionary of Symbols.* Santa Barbara: ABC-CLIO, Inc., 1991.
CITATION: Star, as emblem of war, p. 336.

Lumholtz, Carl. "Decorative Arts of the Huichol Indians." In *Memoirs of the American Museum of Natural History,* Volume III, Part III. New York: The American Museum of Natural History, 1904.

MacGregor, Neil. *A History of the World in 100 Objects.* New York: Viking, 2011.
CITATION: Bird, as winged mediator, p. 569.

Matthews, Boris, translator. *The Herder Dictionary of Symbols.* Wilmette: Chiron Publications, 1994.
CITATIONS: Tiger, p. 199; Owl, p. 143.

Matsumura, Akira, ed. *Daijirin,* 3rd edition. Tokyo: Sanseido, 2006.

Miller, Mary, and Karl Taube. *An Illustrated Dictionary of The Gods and Symbols of Ancient Mexico and the Maya.* London: Thames & Hudson, 2014.
CITATIONS: Teeth, p. 77; Heart, p. 91.

Morgan, Hal. *Symbols of America.* New York: Viking, 1986.

Neubecker, Ottfried. *Heraldry: Sources, Symbols and Meaning.* Maidenhead: McGraw-Hill, 1976.

Page, R.I. *Runes: Reading the Past.* London: British Museum Press, 1987.

Paret, Peter, Beth Irwin Lewis, and Paul Paret. *Persuasive Images: Posters of War and Revolution from the Hoover Institution Archives.* Princeton: Princeton University Press, 1992.

Patch, Diana Craig. *Dawn of Egyptian Art.* New York: The Metropolitan Museum of Modern Art, 2011.

Patterson, Alex. *A Field Guide to Rock Art Symbols of the Greater Southwest.* Boulder: Johnson Books, 1992.

Plutser-Sarno, Alexei. *Russian Criminal Tattoo Encyclopaedia.* Göttingen: Steidl; London: Fuel, 2003.
CITATION: Hand, p. 27.

Pollan, Michael. *Cooked: A Natural History of Transformation.* New York: Penguin Books, 2013.

Ratti, Oscar and Adele Westbrook. *Secrets of the Samurai: The Martial Arts of Feudal Japan.* North Clarendon: Tuttle Publishing, 2011.

Roberts, Allen F. *Animals in African Art.* New York: The Museum for African Art / Prestel, 1995.
CITATION: Dog, p. 31.

Robley, Horatio Gordon. *Moko; or Maori Tattooing.* London: Chapman and Hall, 1896.

Ronnberg, Ami and Kathleen Martin, eds. *The Book of Symbols: Reflections on Archetypal Images.* Cologne and London: Taschen, 2010.
CITATIONS: Chair/Throne, p. 586; Circle, as zero, p. 708.

Rossi, Attilio. *Posters.* London: Paul Hamlyn, 1969.
CITATION: Arrow/Bow, p. 104.

Rothschild, Deborah, Ellen Lupton, and Darra Goldstein. *Graphic Design in the Mechanical Age.* New Haven: Yale University Press, 1998.

Screech, Timon. *Sex and the Floating World: Erotic Images in Japan 1700–1820.* London: Reaktion, 2009.

Shepherd, Rowena and Rupert. *1000 Symbols.* London: Thames and Hudson, 2002.
CITATIONS: Cock, as cockfight, p. 203; Tiger, p. 179; Rat/Mouse, p. 188.

Stapleton, Michael. *The Illustrated Dictionary of Greek and Roman Mythology.* New York: Peter Bedrick Books, 1986.

Stevenson, John. *Yoshitoshi's Women: The Woodblock-Print Series.* Boulder: Avery Press, 1995.

Sutton, Daud. *Islamic Design: A Genius for Geometry.* New York: Walker & Company, 2007.

Tresidder, Jack. *The Complete Dictionary of Symbols.* San Francisco: Chronicle Books, 2005.
CITATIONS: Stone, p. 452; Rat/Mouse, p. 329.

Turner, Bryan S., and Peter Hamilton, eds. *Citizenship: Critical Concepts, Volume 1.* London: Taylor & Francis, 1994.
CITATION: City, p. 212.

Van De Mieroop, Marc. *The Eastern Mediterranean in the Age of Ramesses II.* Hoboken: Wiley-Blackwell, 2009.

Vogel, Susan, and Francine N'Diaye. *African Masterpieces from the Musée de l'Homme.* New York: The Center for African Art and Harry N. Abrams, 1985.
CITATION: Ape/Monkey, as Black Monkey, p. 123.

Werness, Hope B. *The Continuum Encyclopedia of Animal Symbolism in Art.* London: Continuum International Publishing Group, 2004.
CITATION: Lightning, p. 335.

Whitfield, Peter. *Cities of the World: A History in Maps.* Berkeley: University of California Press, 2005.

Whittick, Arnold. *Symbols: Signs and their Meaning and Uses in Design.* London: L. Hill, 1971.
CITATION: Triangle, as hexagram, p. 255.

Wildbur, Peter. *Trademarks: A Handbook of International Designs.* London: Studio Vista, 1966.

Wilkinson, Richard H. *Reading Egyptian Art: a Hieroglyphic Guide to Ancient Egyptian Painting and Sculpture.* London: Thames and Hudson, 1992.
CITATION: Circle, p. 193.

Williams, Geoffrey. *African Designs from Traditional Sources.* New York: Dover Publications, 1971.

In the course of our research we consulted the websites of the following organizations and institutions:

Art Resource
Ashmolean Museum, Oxford
Asia Society, New York
Auckland War Memorial Museum
The British Museum, London
Brooklyn Museum, New York
The J. Paul Getty Trust, Los Angeles
Michael C. Carlos Museum, Emory University, Atlanta
Los Angeles County Museum of Art
The Metropolitan Museum of Art, New York
Münzkabinett Staatliche Museen zu Berlin
Museum of Modern Art, New York
National Museum of the American Indian, Washington, D.C.
The *New York Times*
Pitt Rivers Museum, Oxford
Princeton University Art Museum
Royal Museum for Central Africa, Tervuren
Smithsonian Institution, Washington, D.C.
United States Library of Congress, Washington, D.C.
Victoria and Albert Museum, London
The Walters Art Museum, Baltimore
Yale University Art Gallery, New Haven
Wikipedia

INDEX OF ARTISTS & DESIGNERS

IMAGE CREDITS

TITLE SEQUENCE

p. 2

Monkey netsuke by Masatsugu Kaigyokusai. Japan, 19th century. Collection of Joseph and Elena Kurstin. Photo: Gilles Lorin.

p. 4

The roofline of The House of Terror (*Terror Háza*), Budapest, Hungary. Facade by architect Attila F. Kovács, 2002. Courtesy of Ethan O. Notkin.

p. 5

"Painting the American insignia on airplane wings is a job that Mrs. Irma Lee McElroy, a former office worker, does with precision and patriotic zeal." Photograph by Howard R. Hollem, 1942. Library of Congress, LC-DIG-fsac-1a34899.

p. 6

Paper building blocks with cyrillic letters. Designer and date unknown. Collection of the authors. Photo © 2012 Mark Serr.

p. 7

The Honeycomb Apartments by OFIS arhitekti. Slovenia, 2003–05. Courtesy of OFIS arhitekti. Photo: Tomaz Gregoric.

p. 8

Cheese label for Camembert Parfait. Gabriel Prévot Compiègne, France, 1929. Courtesy of Chronicle Books LLC. From *French Trademarks: The Art Deco Era* © 1991 John Mendenhall.

p. 9

"Robot Moonscape" by Owly Shadow Puppets. United States, 2011. Collection of the authors. Photo © 2012 Mark Serr.

p. 10

Town and Country salt and pepper shakers by Eva Zeisel. Red Wing pottery, c. 1946. Collection of the authors. Photo © 2013 Mark Serr.

TABLE OF CONTENTS

p. 13

Handmade glass eye by J.R. Ballard, early 20th century. Collection of the authors. Photo © 2012 Mark Serr.

FOREWORD

p. 14

Library of Congress, Geography & Map Division, G3382.C5C18 1926 .S33

INTRODUCTION

p. 18

© Erich Lessing/Magnum Photos.

nature

SUN   *p.* 24

1) Collection of the authors. 2) © 2012 Mark Fox. 3) Courtesy of Africa Direct. 4) © The Chambers Gallery, London/Bridgeman Images. 5) Courtesy of Brian Rueb Photography. 6) Collection of the authors. Photo © 2012 Mark Serr. 7) Courtesy of Martinnus Budiarto, flickr.com/photos/marboed. 8) © OOA Fonden, smilingsun.org. Collection of the authors. Photo © 2013 Mark Serr.

MOON   *p.* 28

1) Collection of the authors. Photo © 2012 Mark Serr. 2) Méliès/The Kobal Collection at Art Resource, NY. 3) Library of Congress, LC-DIG-ppmsca-25847. 4) Courtesy of Dover Publications, Inc. From *The Book of Signs*, Rudolf Koch. 5) Courtesy of

Beast Coins. 6) Scala/Art Resource, NY. 7) Lunar and Planetary Institute (NASA), Apollo Image Atlas, AS11-40-5878. 8) Photo: Toby Oxborrow. 9) Courtesy of Hal Morgan.

STAR   *p.* 32

1) Werner Forman/Art Resource, NY. 2) Collection of the authors. Photo © 2012 Mark Serr. 3) © The Image Works. 4) Courtesy of Rex Peteet. 5) Courtesy of History of Science Collections, University of Oklahoma Libraries.

LIGHTNING   *p.* 34

1) Collection of the authors. Photo © 2016 Mark Serr. 2) Walter De Maria, *The Lightning Field*, 1977. Long-term installation, western New Mexico. © 2016 The Estate of Walter De Maria. Photo: John Cliett. Courtesy of Dia Art Foundation, New York. 3) Collection of the authors. 4) Library of Congress, LC-DIG-jpd-02009.

FIRE   *p.* 36

1) The J. Paul Getty Museum, Los Angeles. 2) Photo: Nicholas J. Stankus. 3) Courtesy of René Knip. 4) Erich Lessing/Art Resource, NY. 5) U.S. Department of Energy. 6) © 2002 Mark Fox/BlackDog. 7) © Bodleian Libraries 2016/The Art Archive at Art Resource.

WATER   *p.* 40

1) Library of Congress, LC-USZ62-73320. 2) Collection of the authors. 3) Werner Forman Archive/Bridgeman Images. 4) Collection of the authors. Photo © 2012 Mark Serr. 5) National

Archives, 80-G-418331. 6) Erich Lessing/Art Resource, NY. 7) Photo: bonjourkyoto 8) Courtesy of David Lance Goines. 9) Library of Congress, LC-DIG-highsm-05702.

STONE   *p.* 44

1) Library of Congress, LC-DIG-mat-pc-11906. 2) © Damien Hirst and Science Ltd. All rights reserved/ DACS, London/ARS, NY 2016. Photo: Prudence Cuming Associates Ltd. 3) © The Trustees of the British Museum/Art Resource, NY. 4) Courtesy of Cornell University Library. A.D. White Architectural Photographs, Accession No: 15/5/3090.00976. 5) Courtesy of Dover Publications, Inc. *Symbols, Signs & Signets*, Ernst Lehner. 6) Photo: Edwin Tucker.

TREE   *p.* 48

1) Library of Congress, LC-DIG-jpd-01837. 2) Stephen Album Rare Coins, auction 12, lot 97. 3) Courtesy of Pat Schleger. 4) Reproduced by kind permission of the Syndics of Cambridge University Library. 5) Collection of the authors. Photo © 2016 Mark Serr. 6) Courtesy of Tham & Videgård Arkitekter.

FLOWER   *p.* 52

1) Library of Congress, LC-USZC4-11913. 2) Image copyright © The Metropolitan Museum of Art. Image source: Art Resource, NY. 3) Courtesy of betweenthecovers.com. 4) Ashmolean Museum/ The Art Archive at Art Resource, NY. 5) Collection of the authors. Photo © 2012 Mark Serr. 6) Library of Congress, LC-DIG-jpd-01468.

FRUIT *p.56*
1) Yale University Art Gallery. 2) © 1981 Ester Hernandez, esterhernandez.com. Smithsonian American Art Museum, Washington, DC/Art Resource, NY. 3) Photo © Museum Associates/LACMA. 4) Brooklyn Museum. 5) Collection of the authors. Photo © 2016 Mark Serr. 6) Photo © Museum Associates/ LACMA.

animate

HORSE *p.64*
1) Collection of the authors. Photo © 2013 Mark Serr. 2) © 2012 Mark Fox after a drawing by Josef Hartwig, 1924. 3) Library of Congress, LC-DIG-ds-01299. 4) Yale University Art Gallery. 5) Photo: Mike Sims. 6) Collection of the authors. Photo © 2012 Mark Serr.

BULL *p.68*
1) Yale University Art Gallery. 2) Yale University Art Gallery. 3) Collection of the authors. 4) Collection of the authors. 5) Courtesy of Allan T. Kohl. Art Images for College Teaching, University of Michigan Library.

HORNS/ANTLERS *p.70*
1) Courtesy of Art Chantry. 2) Collection of the authors. 3) Courtesy of Javier Jaén. 4) Bridgeman Images. 5) Library of Congress, LC-USZ62-46963. 6) The J. Paul Getty Museum, Los Angeles. 7) Courtesy of the Hornung Family. Collection of the authors.

SWINE *p.74*
1) Digital Image © The Museum of Modern Art/Licensed by SCALA/ Art Resource, NY. Art © Estate of George Grosz/Licensed by VAGA, New York, NY. 2) © koosen/123RF. 3) United Artists/The Kobal Collection at Art Resource, NY. 4) Collection of the authors. 5) Photos © Chris Rudd, celticcoins.com.

COCK *p.76*
1) Library of Congress, LC-DIG-fsa-8b30547. 2) Digital Image © 2016 Museum Associates/LACMA. Licensed by Art Resource, NY. 3) Image copyright © The Metropolitan Museum of Art. Image source: Art Resource, NY. 4) Public domain. 5) Photo: Joy Russell.

DOG *p.78*
1) © 1996 Greg Clarke. 2) Courtesy of C. Arthur Croyle Archive. 3) Courtesy of George Eastman House, International Museum of Photography and Film. 4) Courtesy of Dover Publications, Inc. *From Design Motifs of Ancient Mexico*, Jorge Enciso. 5) Courtesy of Michael C. Carlos Museum, Emory University. Photo: Bruce M. White, 2006. 6) Library of Congress, WWI Posters, LC-USZC4-10224. 7) Used by permission of Sony Electronics, Inc. 8) Collection of the authors. Photo © 2012 Mark Serr. 9) Collection of the authors.

CAT *p.82*
1) Alinari/Art Resource, NY. 2) Collection of the authors. Photo © 2012 Mark Serr. 3) Courtesy of betweenthecovers.com. 4) Courtesy of Mingei International Museum. Photo: Lynton Gardiner. 5) Courtesy of Chris Irie.

APE/MONKEY *p.84*
1) Collection of Joseph and Elena Kurstin. Photo: Gilles Lorin. 2) Courtesy of Michael Schwab. 3) Courtesy of Africa Direct. 4) Ashmolean Museum, University of Oxford, UK/Bridgeman Images. 5) Courtesy of Dover Publications, Inc. From *Design Motifs of Ancient Mexico*, Jorge Enciso. 6) UCL Library Services, Special Collections.

LION *p.88*
1) Yale University Art Gallery. 2) Brooklyn Museum. 3) Collection of Joseph and Elena Kurstin. Photo: Gilles Lorin. 4) Courtesy of Dover

Publications, Inc. From *Trademark Designs of the World*, Yusaku Kamekura. 5) Yale University Art Gallery. 6) The Walters Art Museum. 7) The J. Paul Getty Museum, Los Angeles. 8) Photo: Paolo Panzeri. 9) MGM/The Kobal Collection at Art Resource, NY.

TIGER *p.92*
1) Princeton University Press/Art Resource, NY. 2) V&A Images, London/Art Resource, NY. 3) Photo © Museum Associates/LACMA. 4) National Archives photo no. 208-AA-12X-21.

ELEPHANT *p.94*
1) Brooklyn Museum. 2) Used by permission. 3) Yale University Art Gallery. 4) Library of Congress Prints and Photographs Division, LC-USZ62-131443.

BEAR *p.96*
1) Image copyright © The Metropolitan Museum of Art. Image source: Art Resource, NY. 2) Collection of the authors. 3) Courtesy Michael Vanderbyl. 4) Photo © Museum Associates/LACMA.

FOX *p.98*
1) Brooklyn Museum. 2) © 2010 Simon Vaeth. 3) Library of Congress, LC-USZ62-99603. 4) Collection of Joseph and Elena Kurstin. Photo: Gilles Lorin. 5) The Kobal Collection at Art Resource, NY.

HARE *p.100*
1) Collection of Joseph and Elena Kurstin. Photo: Gilles Lorin. 2) Courtesy of Dover Publications, Inc. From *Trademark Designs of the Twenties*, Leslie and Marcie Cabarga. 3) Photo: Fred Stimson. 4) Courtesy of Gary Baseman. 5) Collection of the authors. Photo © 2012 Mark Serr. 6) Collection of the authors.

RAT/MOUSE *p.102*
1) Museum of London/The Art Archive at Art Resource, NY.

2) The Walters Art Museum. 3) Image used with permission. © Ed Roth. 4) Photo: Patrick Baldwin. 5) Brooklyn Museum.

BAT *p.104*
1) © The Trustees of the British Museum/Art Resource, NY. 2) Photo: Fred Stimson. 3) Courtesy of Michael C. Carlos Museum, Emory University. Photo: Michael McKelvey. 4) Photo: Daniel Gies. 5) Alinari/Art Resource, NY.

EGG *p.106*
1) Yale University Art Gallery. 2) © The Trustees of the British Museum/Art Resource, NY. 3) Courtesy of David Lance Goines. 4) Alinari/Art Resource, NY. 5) Collection of the authors.

BIRD *p.108*
1) Courtesy of Africa Direct. 2) Kharbine-Tapabor/The Art Archive at Art Resource, NY. 3) © The Trustees of the British Museum/ Art Resource, NY. 4) Courtesy of Leslie Cabarga. 5) Collection of the authors.

EAGLE *p.110*
1) © 1998 Mark Fox/BlackDog. Photo © 2012 Mark Serr. 2) Werner Forman/Art Resource, NY. 3) Courtesy of Beast Coins. 4) Courtesy of Leslie Cabarga. 5) Courtesy of the Hornung Family. Collection of the authors. 6) AZA/ Archive Zabé/Art Resource, NY. 7) Library of Congress, WWI Posters, LC-USZC4-11902.

OWL *p.114*
1) Library of Congress, LC-DIG-highsm-02758. 2) © The Trustees of the British Museum/ Art Resource, NY. 3) Collection of the authors. 4) Yale University Art Gallery.

CROW/RAVEN *p.116*
1) © The Trustees of the British Museum/Art Resource, NY.

2) Courtesy of Donald Ellis Gallery. 3) Collection of the authors. 4) Courtesy of Dennis Crowe. Photo © 2015 Mark Serr. 5) Library of Congress, LC-USZ62-63571.

BEE   *p.118*
1) Courtesy of Tomáš Gabzdil Libertíny and MoMA, NYC. Photo: Raoul Kramer. 2) Courtesy of OFIS arhitekti. Photo: Tomaz Gregoric. 3) Collection of the authors. 4) Collection of the authors. Photo © 2012 Mark Serr.

BUTTERFLY   *p.120*
1) Photo: © aimevera photography. 2) © Demakersvan. Photo: Bas Helbers. Image courtesy of Jeroen Verhoeven and Blain|Southern. 3) © 2012 Mark Fox. 4) Photo: Mackenzie Hussman. 5) Library of Congress, LC-USZ62-90931.

SPIDER   *p.122*
1) Museum für Gestaltung Zurich, Poster Collection. Franz Xaver Jaggy © ZHdK. 2) Image copyright © The Metropolitan Museum of Art. Image source: Art Resource, NY. 3) Collection of the authors. Photo © 2013 Mark Serr. 4) Mingei International Museum/Art Resource, NY. 5) Art © Louise Bourgeois Trust/Licensed by VAGA, New York.

FISH   *p.124*
1) Brooklyn Museum. 2) Courtesy of Michael C. Carlos Museum, Emory University. Photo: Michael McKelvey. 3) Courtesy of Michael C. Carlos Museum, Emory University. Photo: Bruce M. White, 2010. 4) Courtesy of Jay Vigon. 5) The J. Paul Getty Museum, Los Angeles.

OCTOPUS   *p.126*
1) Great Britain Ministry of Information propaganda, Box 3, Hoover Institution Archives. 2) Photo: Matthias Hornung. 3) Courtesy of Charles Spencer Anderson and CustomInk. 4) © The Trustees of the British Museum/Art Resource, NY.

SEASHELL   *p.128*
1) Castle Rock/Columbia/The Kobal Collection at Art Resource, NY. 2) Yale University Art Gallery. Photo: Johan Vipper. 3) Erich Lessing/Art Resource, NY. © F.L.C./ADAGP, Paris/Artists Rights Society (ARS), New York 2016. 4) Digital Image © The Museum of Modern Art/Licensed by SCALA/Art Resource, NY. 5) Collection of the authors. Photo © 2015 Mark Serr.

SNAIL   *p.130*
1) Yale University Art Gallery. 2) Courtesy of Ward Schumaker. 3) Photo © Sara Moiola. 4) Photo © Pierre Bergé & Associés. 5) Courtesy of Dover Publications, Inc. From *Design Motifs of Ancient Mexico*, Jorge Enciso.

FROG/TOAD   *p.132*
1) Photo © Museum Associates/LACMA. 2) Courtesy of the Science Museum, London. 3) Photo © Phyllis Galembo. 4) International Center of Photography. Purchase, with funds provided by the ICP Acquisitions Committee, 2005. © 2016 Artists Rights Society (ARS), New York/VG Bild-Kunst, Bonn. 5) V&A Images, London/Art Resource, NY. 6) Courtesy of Dover Publications, Inc. From *African Designs from Traditional Sources*, Geoffrey Williams. 7) Collection of the authors. Photo © 2014 Mark Serr.

TORTOISE   *p.136*
1) Princeton University Press/Art Resource, NY. 2) Collection of the authors. 3) Image copyright © The Metropolitan Museum of Art. Image source: Art Resource, NY. 4) Photo © Museum Associates/LACMA. 5) © RMN-Grand Palais/Art Resource, NY.

SERPENT   *p.138*
1) Collection of the authors. 2) Courtesy of Dover Publications, Inc. From *Advertising Art in the Art Deco Style*, Theodore Menten.

3) Courtesy of Mark Serr. Photo © 2012 Mark Serr. 4) National Archives and Records Administration, 541335. 5) Library of Congress, LC-USZC4-5315. 6) Collection of the authors. 7) © West 8 Urban Design & Landscape Architecture. 8) Courtesy of Cowan's Auctions. 9) Courtesy of Dover Publications, Inc. From *African Designs from Traditional Sources*, Geoffrey Williams.

human

HAND   *p.144*
1) Ong Soo Beng, ongsb85.blogspot.com. 2) Courtesy of Felix Sockwell. 3) Public domain. 4) Library of Congress, WWI Posters, LC-USZC4-11504. 5) Album/Art Resource, NY. 6) Courtesy of Lies Ros and Rob Schroeder. Collection of the authors. 7) Collection of the authors. Photo © 2012 Mark Serr. 8) Collection of the authors. Photo © 2012 Mark Serr. 9) The Littlejohn Collection, Special Collections at Wofford College.

EYE   *p.148*
1) Collection Merrill C. Berman. Photo: Jim Frank. 2) Digital Image © The Museum of Modern Art/Licensed by SCALA/Art Resource, NY. 3) © 2009 Mark Fox. Photo © 2012 Mark Serr. 4) Collection of the authors. 5) © Aperture Foundation, Inc., Paul Strand Archive. 6) Photo: airliners.nl. 7) Photo: Per Palmkvist Knudsen. 8) Collection of the authors. Photo © 2012 Mark Serr. 9) © 2012 Mark Fox. 10) Courtesy of Michael C. Carlos Museum, Emory University. Photo: Michael McKelvey.

MOUTH/TONGUE   *p.152*
1) © 1970 Brad Holland/Published in the New York Times. 2) Digital Image © The Museum of Modern Art/Licensed by SCALA/Art Resource, NY. © 2016 The Andy Warhol Foundation for the

Visual Arts, Inc./Artists Rights Society (ARS), New York. Rights of Publicity and Persona Rights are used with permission of The Estate of Marilyn Monroe LLC. 3) Brooklyn Museum. 4) Arthur M. Sackler Gallery, Smithsonian Institution, Washington, D.C. Gift of Arthur M. Sackler, S1987.693. 5) Collection of the authors. Photo © 2015 Mark Serr. 6) Collection of the authors. Photo © 2015 Mark Serr. 7) Art by Gary Panter.

TEETH   *p.156*
1) © The Trustees of the British Museum/Art Resource, NY. 2) Library of Congress, LC-USZC4-2715. 3) Collection of the authors. 4) © 1994 Mark Fox/BlackDog. 5) Universal/The Kobal Collection at Art Resource, NY.

FOOT/SHOE   *p.158*
1) Photo © 2012 Nikodem Nijaki. 2) © CULTNAT, Dist. RMN-GP/Art Resource, NY. 3) Yale University Art Gallery. 4) Library of Congress, WWI Posters, LC-USZC4-9853. 5) Galerie Janette Ostier, Paris, France/Bridgeman Images. 6) Collection of the authors. Photo © 2013 Mark Serr. 7) Erich Lessing/Art Resource, NY.

HEART   *p.162*
1) Courtesy of James Victore. 2) © The Trustees of the British Museum/Art Resource, NY. 3) © 2013 Mark Fox and Angie Wang. 4) Brooklyn Museum 5) © Historic England/Bridgeman Images. 6) © The Trustees of the British Museum/Art Resource, NY.

HAIR   *p.166*
1) Poster GE 189, Poster Collection, Hoover Institution Archives. 2) Courtesy of California Historical Society, FN-08023. 3) Library of Congress, LC-USZ62-119411. 4) Yale University Art Gallery 5) Erich Lessing/Art Resource, NY. 6) Dylan by Milton Glaser © 1967. Courtesy of Milton Glaser.

NIMBUS *p.170*
1) V&A Images, London/Art Resource, NY. © 2012 Artists Rights Society (ARS), New York/VG Bild-Kunst, Bonn. 2) Library of Congress, WWI Posters, LC-USZC4-9726. 3) Library of Congress, Edward S. Curtis Collection, LC-USZC4-8927. 4) Collection of the authors. Photo © 2012 Mark Serr. 5) Library of Congress, LC-USZ62-18086.

TWINS *p.172*
1) Library of Congress, LC-DIG-ppmsca-27682. 2) Collection of the authors. Photo © 2012 Mark Serr. 3) Collection of the authors. 4) Collection of the authors. 5) Collection of the authors. Photo © 2012 Mark Serr. 6) Photo © Anatoly Pronin/Bridgeman Images.

man-made

WHEEL *p.178*
1) Beinecke Rare Book and Manuscript Library, Yale University. 2) Courtesy of Leslie Cabarga. 3) Alfredo Dagli Orti/The Art Archive at Art Resource, NY. 4) Courtesy of Leslie Cabarga. 5) Photo © Museum Associates/LACMA. 6) Margaret Bourke-White/Getty Images. 7) Library of Congress, Prints & Photographs Division. Dr. Alice S. Kandell Collection of Sikkim Photographs, LC-DIG-ppmsca-30889; and LC-DIG-ppmsca-31642. 8) Brooklyn Museum. 9) City of Amsterdam, design by Dsgnfrm and Razormind.

ARROW/BOW *p.182*
1) Courtesy of George Lois. 2) Courtesy of Dover Publications, Inc. From *Trademark Designs of the World*, Yusaku Kamekura. 3) © 1998 Mark Fox. 4) Image copyright © The Metropolitan Museum of Art. Image source: Art Resource, NY. 5) © 2015 Mark Fox. 6) Collection of the authors. 7) © The Trustees of the British Museum/Art Resource, NY.

HAMMER *p.186*
1) © 1995 Mark Fox/BlackDog. Photo © 2016 Mark Serr. 2) Collection of the authors. Photo © 2016 Mark Serr. 3) Collection of the authors. 4) V&A Images, London/Art Resource, NY. 5) With permission from the Senator Ervin Library and Museum on the campus of Western Piedmont Community College, Morganton, NC.

DOOR/GATE *p.188*
1) Library of Congress, LC-DIG-ppmsc-05229. 2) Warner Brothers/The Kobal Collection at Art Resource, NY. 3) Courtesy of the U.S. National Archives and Records Administration. 4) Collection of the authors. 5) © Sean Pavone/123RF. 6) © GophObservation/500px.

CITY *p.192*
1) Digital Image © The Museum of Modern Art/Licensed by SCALA/Art Resource, NY. 2) Yale University Art Gallery. 3) The Miriam and Ira D. Wallach Division of Art, Prints and Photographs: Photography Collection, The New York Public Library. 4) Reproduced by permission of Letterform Archive. 5) Yale University Art Gallery. 6) The Walters Art Museum. 7) © Pavel Dvorak/500px.

CHAIR/THRONE *p.196*
1) Collection Merrill C. Berman. 2) Image copyright © The Metropolitan Museum of Art. Image source: Art Resource, NY. 3) Courtesy of Matthias Hofmann. 4) Brooklyn Museum. 5) Library of Congress, LC-USZ62-35631.

MIRROR *p.198*
1) Library of Congress, LC-USZ62-139542. 2) © The Trustees of the British Museum/Art Resource, NY. 3) Photo © Museum Associates/LACMA. 4) BuzzFeed. 5) Photo © Museum Associates/LACMA. 6) Courtesy of Dover Publications, Inc. From *The Book of Signs*, Rudolf Koch. 7) Columbia/Frank Cronenweth/The Kobal Collection at Art Resource, NY.

BREAD *p.202*
1) Library of Congress, LC-USZ62-22190. 2) Courtesy of Yanase Takashi Memorial Anpanman Museum Promotion Foundation. Used by permission of Froebel-Kan Co., Ltd. 3) Photo © Museum Associates/LACMA. 4) Reprinted with permission of the Corita Art Center, Immaculate Heart Community, Los Angeles. 5) The Walters Art Museum. 6) bpk, Berlin/Museum für Islamische Kunst, Staatliche Museen zu Berlin/Photo: John Kramer/Art Resource, NY. 7) Library of Congress, LC-USZC4-11903.

BOOK *p.206*
1) Courtesy of Soler y Llach, soleryllach.com. 2) © The Trustees of the British Museum/Art Resource, NY. 3) Collection of the authors. 4) © 2005 Mark Fox/BlackDog. 5) Photo: F. Nagel, Orange-ear.de.

AIRPLANE *p.208*
1) Courtesy of Swann Auction Galleries. © 2012 Artists Rights Society (ARS), New York/VG Bild-Kunst, Bonn. 2) National Air and Space Museum Archives, Smithsonian Institution, WEB12227-2011. 3) Rago Arts and Auction Center, ragoarts.com. 4) Collection Merrill C. Berman. Photo: Jim Frank. Art © Estate of Aleksandr Rodchenko/RAO, Moscow/VAGA, New York. 5) Collection of the authors. Photo © 2012 Mark Serr. 6) Collection of the authors. 7) Photo © 2011 Kevin Dickert. 8) Library of Congress, Exit Art's "Reactions" Exhibition Collection, LC-DIG-ppmsca-01687.

abstract

CROSS *p.214*
1) State Russian Museum, St. Petersburg, Russia/Bridgeman Images. 2) © 2012 Mark Fox. 3) Viking Ship Museum, Oslo, Norway/Bridgeman Images. 4) Library of Congress, Manuscript Division, Theodore Roosevelt Papers. 5) © 2012 Mark Fox after a sketch by Garrick Mallery, 1893. 6) Library of Congress, LC-DIG-prokc-21387. 7) Photo: Jay Anderson. 8) Courtesy of Ethan O. Notkin. 9) Princeton University Press/Art Resource, NY.

CIRCLE *p.218*
1) Untitled by anonymous, near Sanganer, India, 2005 from *Tantra Song: Tantric Painting from Rajasthan*, edited by Franck André Jamme, Siglio, 2011. Image courtesy of Franck André Jamme and Siglio. 2) Collection of the authors. 3) © 1985 Marilyn Bridges. 4) Collection of the authors. 5) VUFKU/The Kobal Collection at Art Resource, NY. 6) © Museum Associates/LACMA. 7) Kharbine-Tapabor/The Art Archive at Art Resource, NY.

CONCENTRIC CIRCLES *p.222*
1) Courtesy History of Science Collections, University of Oklahoma Libraries. 2) Collection of the authors. 3) © Ali Jarekji/Reuters Pictures. 4) © 2012 Mark Fox. 5) Collection of the authors. Photo © 2012 Mark Serr.

SQUARE *p.224*
1) Collection Merrill C. Berman. Photo: Jim Frank. 2) © Kamran Diba/Aga Khan Award for Architecture. 3) Courtesy of Mike and Maaike. 4) © 2012 Mark Fox. 5) Collection of the authors. 6) Collection of the authors. Photo © 2012 Mark Serr. 7) Dublin City Gallery, The Hugh Lane, Ireland/Bridgeman Images. © 2016 The Josef and Anni Albers Foundation/Artists Rights Society (ARS), New York.

TRIANGLE *p.228*
1) Library of Congress, LC-DIG-ppmsca-03954. 2) Collection of the authors. Photo © 2012 Mark Serr. 3) Image copyright © The

Metropolitan Museum of Art. Image
source: Art Resource, NY. 4) The
New York Public Library. 5) © 2015
Mark Fox. 6) Library of Congress,
LC-DIG-ppmsca-09504. 7) Photo:
Shiho Tsukada.

LOZENGE   *p. 232*
1) EO.0.0.43146, collection MRAC
Tervuren; Photo: R. Asselberghs,
MRAC Tervuren ©. 2) The Beinecke
Rare Book & Manuscript Library,
Yale University. 3) Fine Arts Museums of San Francisco. Gift of Marcia
and John Friede. 4) Collection of the
authors.

SPIRAL   *p. 234*
1) Collection Merrill C. Berman.
Photo: Jim Frank. 2) Public domain.
3) Photo: Nico Potgieter. 4) Alastair
Northedge, Samarra Archaeological
Survey. 5) Public domain. 6) Gianni
Dagli Orti/The Art Archive at Art
Resource, NY. 7) Public domain.

TRISKELE   *p. 238*
1) Courtesy of David Lance Goines.
2) Collection of the authors. 3) bpk,
Berlin/Münzkabinett der Staatli-
chen Museen zu Berlin/Photo: Dirk
Sonnenwald/Art Resource, NY. 4)
Courtesy of Dover Publications, Inc.
From *Trademarks: A Handbook of
International Designs*, Peter Wildbur.

SWASTIKA   *p. 240*
1) © The Trustees of the British
Museum/Art Resource, NY. 2)
Fernie and District Historical
Society, no. 972. 3) Manuel Cohen/
The Art Archive at Art Resource,
NY. 4) Photo: Rex Features. 5) Public
domain. 6) Library of Congress, LC-
DIG-ppmsca-18744.

IMPRINT
p. 256
Illustration for San Francisco Center
for the Book by Ward Schumaker,
2015. Courtesy of Ward Schumaker.

colophon

DTL DOCUMENTA AND DOCUMENTA SANS

Our book's principal text faces are Documenta and Documenta Sans,
designed by Frank E. Blokland and issued by the Dutch Type Library.
In his *Elements of Typographic Style*, Robert Bringhurst describes
Documenta as a "sturdy open text face" with an "equally unpretentious
and well-made sanserif companion." These faces were released in 1993
and 1997, respectively.

BLENDER PRO

The principal display face is Blender Pro, a geometric sans serif
designed by Nik Thoenen and released under Gestalten Fonts in 2003.
Blender is based on the typeface Gridnik—a sans serif monoline with
chamfered corners—designed by Wim Crouwel in 1974 for typewriter
manufacturer Olivetti.

DTL PROKYON

German type designer Erhard Kaiser conceived Prokyon as a sans serif
typeface with classical proportions and modern forms. His aim to
achieve *formreduktion* or "simplification of shapes" of common letters
is particularly apparent in the lowercase *a, d, m, n, p, q and r*. Prokyon is
equipped with three different kinds of numerals and traditional small
caps, and was issued by the Dutch Type Library in 2000.

HTF KNOCKOUT

Knockout is a sans serif display face designed by Jonathan Hoefler and
Tobias Frere-Jones, released under Hoefler & Frere-Jones in 1994. This
robust family of thirty-two cuts includes nine widths and four weights.
We feature FullSumo, Welterweight, and Junior Welterweight on the
cover of our book.

OBLONG

Our cover design also includes Oblong, a display face designed by René
Knip and Janno Hahn. Knip's interest in architecture is evident in the
typeface's generous proportions. According to Knip, "The massive
letters become standalone objects that can be mounted on roofs and
walls. An exceptional coherence between text and architecture is
achieved." Issued under the foundry Arktype in 2012.

We are deeply grateful to our photographer, Mark Serr, for contributing to this project over the course of many years. His ability to transform the banal into the photographic sublime borders on alchemy.

We would also like to extend our thanks to Steven Heller for writing the book's foreword, and to our editor at The Monacelli Press, Alan Rapp, for his insights and guidance. (And patience!) Additional thanks to Madeleine Compagnon, editorial assistant.

We are indebted to our many contributors. In particular, we would like to thank Merrill C. Berman and Joseph and Elena Kurstin for letting us reproduce work from their personal collections.

The following curators and scholars generously shared their expertise: Dr. Anne-Marie Bouttiaux, Royal Museum for Central Africa, Tervuren, Belgium; Dr. Kendall Brown, Professor of Asian Art History, California State University Long Beach; Dr. Alexa Küter, Münzkabinett Staatliche Museen zu Berlin, Germany; and Timon Screech, Professor of the History of Art, School of Oriental and African Studies, University of London.

Nami Kurita and Heidi Reifenstein provided research and translations; Jennifer Belt and Peter Rohowsky at Art Resource in New York contributed additional research assistance. Cate Tam read the finished manuscript and noted errors and inconsistencies. Thank you all!

Finally, we are grateful to California College of the Arts for partially funding this project through the awarding of faculty enrichment grants. The college's ongoing support of our work is appreciated.